Detroit Architecture

Katharine Mattingly Meyer
Editor

Martin C. P. McElroy
Editor, Revised Edition

With an Introduction by
W. Hawkins Ferry, Hon. A.I.A.

Detroit
Architecture
A.I.A. Guide

Revised Edition

Wayne State University Press
Detroit

03   02   01   8   7   6

Library of Congress Cataloging in Publication Data

Main entry under title:
Detroit architecture.

Includes index.
1.   Architecture — Michigan — Detroit — Guide-books.
2.   Detroit — Buildings — Guide-books. I. Meyer, Katharine
Mattingly. II. McElroy, Martin C. P. III. American Institute of
Architects. Detroit Chapter.
NZ735.D4D4 1980 917.74'340443 80-13226
ISBN 0-8143-1651-4 (pbk.)

The American Institute of Architects
Detroit Chapter

Contents

Detroit Architecture to 1971

Detroit Architecture, 1971-1980

Picture Credits

Foreword

Prepared under the sponsorship of the Detroit Chapter, the American Institute of Architects, this is the story of Detroit as told by its architecture—an architecture that only developed a distinctive style with the advent of the automobile when Albert Kahn combined form and function to accommodate the industry that is synonymous with the city's name.

The architect, student, or tourist will find examples, arranged in 11 geographical walking or driving tours, of the work of some of the world's most celebrated designers, as well as of many highly skilled and talented local architectural firms. Not intended as a critique, the contents were selected as representative of the historical and contemporary architecture of the area—judgments are left to the individual.

The material in this guide was drawn largely from the book by W. Hawkins Ferry, *The Buildings of Detroit: A History* (Wayne State University Press, 1968), and is reproduced with his permission.* Mr. Ferry also acted as advisor in the selection of recently constructed buildings from lists submitted by members of the Detroit Chapter, AIA. His years of research and deep interest in the architecture of Detroit thus form the backbone of the guidebook.

Craig Farley prepared the excellent area maps and graphic design, and Charles H. Elam provided editorial assistance. Appreciation is also extended to the architects of Detroit and their staffs, and to photographers, public agencies, and the publisher for their contributions, suggestions, and cooperation.

Finally, this book is the responsibility of a committee of the Detroit Chapter, AIA: Joseph L. Fleshner, Charles T. McCafferty, and Charles H. MacMahon Jr., FAIA, chairman.

K. M. M.
Detroit, 1971

*Mr. Ferry also generously furnished the majority of the photographs, of which many valuable historical ones do not reflect subsequent alterations, notably suffered by several churches when Woodward Avenue was widened in the 1930's.

Foreword to the Revised Edition

More new construction is now in progress in Detroit than ever before in the city's history, including the heyday of the 1920's. Such a claim normally would be verified by measures of area or money or material. Instead, this new edition of *Detroit Architecture: A.I.A. Guide* is offered as dramatic visual proof of Detroit's resurgence in building.

Many kinds of people are making Detroit's architecture happen—financiers, politicians, bureaucrats. (Henry Ford II is a particularly prominent example.) More than ever, they—and the general public—expect the architect to produce architecture worth remembering, work that is a fitting celebration of a large urban area's efforts to rebuild itself. How well architects are responding is demonstrated in the examples cited in this book.

The Wayne State University Press invited, and the Detroit Chapter of the American Institute of Architects assented to, the revision of the original *Detroit Architecture: A.I.A. Guide* (1971), so that samples of the architecture put in place in the past nine years could be included.

But this guidebook is only a survey. Readers are encouraged to discover on their own the many outstanding examples of new uses for old buildings, new futures for old sites, and bright approaches to inventive development everywhere—all further indications, as this book suggests, that architecture is playing an important role in Detroit's renaissance.

Special thanks are due to TMP Associates and to the Detroit Chapter, A.I.A., for their support and encouragement in the completion of this project. Grateful acknowledgment is also made to the many photographers who contributed their work and to the architects who generously supplied photographs and information. Balthazar Korab, the noted architectural photographer, in addition to donating a number of other photographs for the book, provided a cover photograph particularly expressive of Detroit's new appeal as a city for people on foot.

M. C. P. M.
Detroit, 1980

8

Introduction by W. Hawkins Ferry

Detroit is known throughout the world chiefly as an industrial city. The secret of its success has been its ability for sustained growth. As old industries died out, new ones were rapidly developed. The fur trade, the principal means of livelihood during the 18th century, was supplanted by the lumber, iron and steel industries in the 19th, and in the 20th century the automobile industry came to the fore.

The 18th century pioneer village of log cabins surrounded by a wooden stockade was wiped out in the disastrous fire of 1805. It was only at the beginning of the 19th century that the stabilization of the frontier encouraged settlers in appreciable numbers to migrate from the East. Then began the phenomenal growth of population that has continued unabated to the present day, augmented by emigration from Europe and migrations from the South.

The rapidly expanding town of the 19th century mirrored a bewildering succession of architectural styles that were generated in the East. Unfortunately, not much of this 19th century Detroit remains. The flat topography of the city facilitated mobility and made it difficult to maintain the character of neighborhoods. The lines between commercial, industrial, and residential districts were often blurred. In the outward thrust of population, old buildings were replaced or allowed to deteriorate.

It is the purpose of this guidebook to point out outstanding surviving examples of the city's varied architectural past, at the same time keeping abreast of current architectural developments.

The early 19th century saw Detroit a serene Neo-Classic town abounding in temple-front porticoes and bristling with church steeples. All that remains of this period are Saints Peter and Paul's R.C. Church, and the Chene, Sibley, and Trowbridge houses. Into this classical milieu the Jordan brothers of Hartford, Connecticut, and Gordon W. Lloyd of England introduced the somber melancholy of the Gothic Revival. Surviving are the Jordans' Fort Street Presbyterian and Saint John's P.E. Churches, and Lloyd's Christ P.E. and Central Methodist Churches, and his Thomas A. Parker house, opposite the former on Jefferson Avenue.

The two architectural giants of the late 19th century were

Gordon W. Lloyd and Mortimer L. Smith. Both became intrigued with the use of cast iron. Still surviving are Lloyd's Parker Building, faced with superimposed arcades of cast iron, and Smith's Gothic Woodward Avenue Baptist Church, supported on the interior with tall, slender iron columns.

All of the Second Empire Mansardic mansions have disappeared, but still intact are Lloyd's David Whitney Jr. house in the Romanesque Revival style and Colonel Frank J. Hecker's French chateau by Scott, Kamper and Scott, both on Woodward Avenue. Two other late Victorian monuments, both by Wilson Eyre Jr. of Philadelphia, are the Detroit Club in the Romanesque Revival style and the Charles L. Freer house in the shingle style. Two outstanding Romanesque Revival churches on Woodward Avenue are the First Presbyterian Church by Mason and Rice, and the First Congregational Church by J. Lyman Faxon of Boston. The Bagley Fountain in downtown Detroit was designed by the great master of the Romanesque Revival, Henry Hobson Richardson himself.

The full-blown Renaissance architecture of the Beaux-Arts tradition came to fruition in Detroit at the turn of the century. Notable examples are the Wayne County Building by John Scott, the Detroit Public Library by Cass Gilbert, and the Detroit Institute of Arts by Paul Philippe Cret. McKim, Mead and White, the leading exponents of the Beaux-Arts tradition in New York, were the architects of the Peoples State Bank, now the Manufacturers National Bank of Detroit. Louis Kamper followed the Italian Renaissance tradition in his designs of the James Burgess Book house and his own house, both in the Indian Village district of Detroit.

The great eclectic mansions of the Age of Elegance were built in Grosse Pointe, on the shores of Lake Saint Clair, in the early years of the present century. Many have since been torn down because of increasing taxes and maintenance costs. Remaining examples are the Russell A. Alger and Mrs. Henry Stephens houses by Charles Adams Platt, the Roy D. Chapin house by John Russell Pope, the Emory W. Clark house by Hugh T. Keyes, the Mrs. Horace E. Dodge house (Rose Terrace) by Horace Trumbauer, and the Alvan Macauley and Edsel B. Ford houses by Albert Kahn.

In the 20th century the architectural role of Detroit was reversed from being a follower to being a leader in architectural
trends. The city had grown to be the fourth largest in the country,

and in the boom period of the twenties, building activity rivaled that of New York and Chicago. Considerable architectural talent was attracted to the city. It was in the twenties that Smith, Hinchman and Grylls (Mortimer L. Smith's successors) built the principal downtown skyscrapers.

A marked interest in modern design trends manifested itself early in the century by the formation of the Detroit Society of Arts and Crafts. Affiliated with this movement, Mary Chase Stratton, a ceramist, established the Pewabic Pottery. George Gough Booth, publisher of the Detroit *News,* was the leader of the movement, and his involvement led to the establishment of the Cranbrook Foundation in Bloomfield Hills. Eliel Saarinen, famed Finnish architect, was the designer of various Cranbrook buildings; as director of the Cranbrook Academy of Art, he provided a vital stimulus to the architectural and artistic life of the area.

Albert Kahn, trained in the office of Mason and Rice, began his career as an eclectic architect. He designed many private residences, including that of George G. Booth in Bloomfield Hills (Cranbrook House). He also built many Detroit office buildings in the tradition of Daniel H. Burnham of Chicago. These include the National Bank, General Motors, and Fisher Buildings. Early in his career, however, Kahn's practical bent was recognized and he was called upon to be the architect of many of the factories required for the nascent automobile industry. Concerning himself with problems of structure, circulation, and natural lighting, he soon revolutionized the entire field of industrial architecture, creating an entirely new concept of the factory. He was responsible for the vast complexes of the Ford Highland Park and the Ford River Rouge Plants, and his Dodge Half-Ton Truck Plant and De Soto Press Shop have become famous for the bold simplicity of their designs.

After World War II, Detroiters bent their energies toward the revitalization of the inner city. The riverfront Civic Center was developed from the original plans by Saarinen, Saarinen and Associates, and is now being brought to completion. A freeway system was built linking the city with a network of state and national highways. A new Medical Center was started in the so-called Woodward Corridor, and a new campus was developed for Wayne State University near the Cultural Center. Perhaps the most outstanding building on the campus is the McGregor Memorial Conference Center by Minoru Yamasaki, who also 11 designed several other buildings for the university, as well as the Michigan Consolidated Gas Company Building in downtown Detroit and the Reynolds Metals Building in Southfield.

Lafayette Park and Elmwood Park, vast urban redevelopment projects, were begun after World War II in an effort to counteract the exodus to the suburbs by providing convenient and attractive living quarters close to the heart of the city. Of particular interest in this area are the high-rise apartments and town houses by Mies van der Rohe and a high-rise apartment house by Birkerts and Straub, known as 1300 East Lafayette.

Among other post-war manifestations were vast shopping centers in suburban areas. Outstanding are the J. L. Hudson Company's Northland, Eastland, and Westland, designed by Victor Gruen Associates of Los Angeles.

The automobile industry attained its ultimate expression of controlled industrial environment with the General Motors Technical Center in Warren. Here Eero Saarinen carried to a dramatic climax the precepts formulated by Albert Kahn, at the same time providing a springboard for a career that was to win him international acclaim.

Early Detroit

The Great Lakes area, with inhospitable forests and extremes of climate, was long ignored by European explorers and might have remained indefinitely in its primordial condition had not the French, beginning with Cartier, desired to discover the legendary passage to the Western Sea and the Indies. It was this vision that lured them up the St. Lawrence to the Great Lakes and the Northwest. By 1669 the French were beginning to invade the Lower Peninsula of Michigan.

In the meantime English traders became serious competitors in the fur trade, and to prevent them from reaching the upper lakes, Daniel Greysolon Sieur Duluth built Fort St. Joseph at the head of the St. Clair River in 1686. In 1690 Fort de Buade was erected at Michilimackinac, and in 1691 a new Fort St. Joseph was built 25 miles up the St. Joseph River from where La Salle had established Fort Miami at its mouth in 1679. Michilimackinac was the most important place in the West.

From 1694 to 1698 Antoine de la Mothe Cadillac was commandant of Michilimackinac, which grew from a small missionary outpost to a busy trading center. Missionaries became distressed at the way their Indian charges were demoralized by the ample supply of brandy provided by white traders. As a result, in 1696 Louis XIV ordered all Frenchmen except missionaries to leave the upper country. Thus in 1698 Forts de Buade and St. Joseph were abandoned. Cadillac was not one to stand idly by and watch New France crumble. In Paris he persuaded the king to allow him to establish a new post on the strait between Lake St. Clair and Lake Erie which, he argued, was necessary to hold the English in check and to subdue the Iroquois.

On 23 July 1701 Cadillac reached the Detroit River. Soon he located an ideal site for a fort at the narrowest stretch of the river, where there was a level expanse of ground at the tip of a 40-foot clay bank, and a small creek ran parallel to the river, then turned and joined it. On this peninsula of high ground Cadillac built *Fort Pontchartrain du Detroit* (Fort Pontchartrain of the Strait). The fort was about 200 feet square with bastions at each corner. There was a large gate toward the river and a small one to the west. The most prominent buildings were the church, the priest's, Cadillac's, and Lieut. Tonty's houses, a warehouse, and two guard houses. The fort was located in an area bounded today by the southern side of Jefferson Avenue and Griswold, Larned, and Shelby Streets in downtown Detroit.

During the 18th century Detroit grew very slowly and remained a small outpost in the wilderness. Too few Frenchmen found the West attractive enough to settle there, and so the West was largely the domain of shiftless coureurs de bois.

The foresight of Cadillac in establishing Detroit had kept the French in control of the Great Lakes, but the more enterprising British were becoming disturbingly competitive, and in the conflict that developed to decide who would control the American continent, they had the advantage of a much greater population. After the fall of Quebec and Montreal, Canada was surrendered in 1760 to the British, who soon occupied all the French posts in the Northwest, including Detroit.

Although the French settlers and their English rulers in Detroit were friendly, British traders swarmed over the country, cheating Indians and robbing them of their furs. The Ottawa Chief Pontiac was so incensed that he conceived a plan for obliterating Detroit. In 1763 he held the little stockaded town in a state of siege for five months. It was only due to the assistance of the loyal French and the good judgment of Commandant Major Henry Gladwin that Detroit survived and Pontiac finally offered to make peace.

After the tribulations of the Pontiac War the English deemed it necessary to maintain a large garrison permanently. In 1764 a parade ground and barracks were added to the west of the town. At the beginning of the Revolutionary War, between 200 and 300 soldiers occupied this enclosure, and during the war it was used partly to hold prisoners of war. British Detroit became the base of operations for murderous raids into the western country by both whites and Indians. In 1779, apprehensive of the American victories of Col. George Rogers Clark, Capt. Richard B. Lernoult built a northern fort, later called Fort Detroit, and after the War of 1812, Fort Shelby.

When the Revolution terminated in 1783 the Americans were pledged by treaty to compensate for property taken from exiled Tories. Since the war weary American people failed to carry out their part of the bargain, the British government retaliated by withholding the surrender of Detroit, and the city remained under Canadian rule until 1796, when on 11 July the British hauled down the Union Jack and the American flag was raised.

Two days later Col. John Francis Hamtramck arrived at Detroit and took command with a garrison of 400 men. At last, 13 years after the ratification of the Treaty of Paris, Michigan became a part of the United States.

Under the American flag Detroit was located in an area designated by the Ordinance of 1787 as the Northwest Territory. Out of this area were eventually carved the states of Ohio, Indiana, Illinois, Michigan, Wisconsin, and part of Minnesota. By 1798 the population of the Northwest Territory was sufficiently large for the establishment of a territorial legislature, which met first at Cincinnati and later at Chillicothe. Wayne County was entitled to 3 elected members of the new assembly. In 1802 one of these members, a young lawyer named Solomon Sibley, procured the passage of an act at Chillicothe incorporating the "Town of Detroit," the county seat

In 1805 a bill enacted in Washington created Michigan Territory, which included approximately the present area of the Lower Peninsula and a small portion of the Upper Peninsula. The territory was to be administered by a governor and 3 judges. President Jefferson appointed William Hull of Massachusetts as governor and Augustus B. Woodward of Washington as chief justice.

Detroit was completely destroyed by fire on 11 June 1805 and the new territorial rulers arrived to find nothing left of their capital but charred debris and a few tottering stone chimneys. It was fortunate that fate brought Woodward to Detroit at this grave moment in its history. A man of extraordinary intellectual curiosity, he was aware of the latest developments in city planning and had the imagination to visualize a model metropolis of the future on the site of the ruined frontier post. He was a friend of Jefferson and knew Major L'Enfant, who was responsible for the plan of Washington.

Woodward's Detroit plan was not merely a copy of L'Enfant's Washington plan, a gridiron system of streets overlaid on radial diagonals, for Woodward's was based on a hexagon, divided into 12 sections, which could be repeated ad infinitum. There were principal north-south and east-west parkway boulevards 200 feet wide, secondary diagonal avenues 120 feet wide, interconnecting streets, and circles or circuses and other open spaces. In 1805-1806 Congress authorized the platting of the new plan. The work of surveying and laying out the streets proceeded slowly. Unfortunately, uncooperative land owners prevented all but a fragment of the original plan from being   15 carried out. However, we are indebted to Woodward for the broad avenues and open spaces which today give downtown Detroit a distinctive quality. The area bounded by Michigan and Monroe Aves., Randolph St., and Adams and Cass Aves. represents a small part of one hexagon which was to have a full circle Grand Circus Park in the center.

The dawn of 1815 found Detroit prostrate from the ravages of the War of 1812, but the coming of peace brought new hope. President Madison appointed Lewis Cass governor of Michigan Territory. During the 15 years of his administration Cass converted a wilderness outpost into the capital of an empire.

The Ohio River was a natural thoroughfare for the settlers who began to move west at the beginning of the 19th century. Thus the main stream of immigration at first flowed past Michigan. To reach Michigan, settlers from the East came along the Mohawk Trail to Buffalo where they embarked on sailing vessels for Detroit. The first steamship on the Great Lakes was *Walk-in-the-Water,* named after a Wyandotte chief. Its initial trip from Buffalo to Detroit was made in 1818, thus opening an era of steam navigation.

Also in 1818 a government land office was opened in Detroit and recently surveyed land was offered for sale to the public. Settlers whose wagons were loaded with farm implements and household goods needed roads to reach their new land in the interior of Michigan. Governor Cass appealed to the federal government for financial aid, and by the 1820's roads began fanning out in all directions from Detroit. New towns sprang up along these routes. In the 1820's when the English and the Indians were no longer considered a serious threat, Fort Shelby and the stockade around Detroit were dismantled. At last the town was breaking out of its chrysalis, the frontier era was drawing to a close, and ahead lay a time of peaceful growth and prosperity.

It was not until after the completion of the Erie Canal in 1825 that the full tide of immigrants reached Michigan. By 1835 two stagecoaches a week made the round trip from Detroit to Chicago, and during 1836 as many as 2,000 arrived at Detroit in a single day on steamships and sailing vessels. By 1860 the population of the city was more than 45,000.

The subsequent phenomenal commercial and industrial growth of Detroit, especially in the automotive field, is reflected in the comments that follow.

Detroit
Architecture
to 1971

*(Note: Date cited after architect's name indicates year of
project's completion or anticipated completion.)*

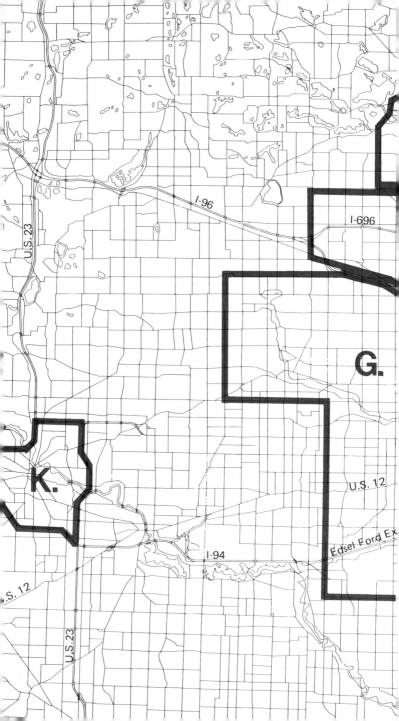

DETROIT AREA

A. Downtown Detroit

Civic Center

Ever since the founding of Detroit in 1701 the magnificent frontage on the Detroit River has been used mainly for commercial purposes. It was reform-minded Mayor Hazen S. Pingree who in 1890 first suggested a civic center be located at the foot of Woodward Ave. For many years the idea was bandied about while the area continued to deteriorate. Finally, after World War I some progress was made. A plan was developed to build a river front civic center to serve as a war memorial. In 1924 *Eliel Saarinen,* then teaching at the University of Michigan, was commissioned by the AIA to draw up a design. He envisioned a domical memorial hall with a long wing to house an exposition hall and convention auditorium; included was a soaring tower, reminiscent of his Chicago *Tribune* tower design. In 1925 the voters approved the project, but no progress was made for lack of funds.

After World War II the civic center idea was revived. In 1947 *Saarinen, Saarinen & Assoc.* were engaged by the City Plan Commission to develop a new plan and act as consultants. Abandoning the old concepts of monumentality and symmetry, they grouped public buildings around a landscaped plaza facing the river. The scheme included a city-county building, a circular convention hall, an auditorium and music hall, and four government buildings for federal, state, and local functions.

In 1950 the first unit of the Civic Center, Veterans Memorial Hall, was completed, fulfilling the dream for a war memorial. Designed by *Harley, Ellington & Day* and begun before the *Saarinens* were called in, it was incorporated in their plan.

The *Saarinens* visualized a round convention hall at the western end of the Civic Center, but industrial leaders and automobile executives pointed out there was no place to hold the National Automobile Show. They suggested an exhibit hall be added to the convention hall and were willing to back it with financial support. Mayor Albert E. Cobo enthusiastically accepted their ideas; with city aid, Cobo Hall was born (A-6).

A-1 Michigan Consolidated Gas Co.
Minoru Yamasaki & Assoc. and *Smith, Hinchman & Grylls.* 1963.
1 Woodward Ave. (BK)

A distinctive building that rises from a marble platform like something out of the *Arabian Nights*. A 30-foot high glass enclosed lobby with marble columns is reflected in exterior pools. At night sparkling blue lights suspended from the lobby ceiling create a jewel-like effect, and on special occasions, gas jets flicker over the pools, illuminating a bronze ballerina by Giacomo Manzù.

Avoiding the monotony imposed by standardized products, *Yamasaki* gave an interesting form and texture to the exterior walls by the use of precast prestressed concrete panels, 2 stories high. They were joined at the centers of windows, forming extended hexagonal openings, designed to emphasize verticality and avoid acrophobia, even though the glass extends nearly to the floor. The building terminates with a lacy grille encompassing floors 27 and 28.

A-2 Guardian Building.
Smith, Hinchman & Grylls. 1929
500 Griswold. (L-A)

One of its most unusual architectural features is the use of the stepped or notched arch, suggested by the natural way of piling brick without adding curved or molded forms. The influence of early 20th century Dutch architecture is apparent in the fine brickwork, there are reminders as well of the skyscraper designs of *Ralph Walker* and *Raymond Hood* in New York, and the Arts and Crafts movement and the Paris Exposition of Decorative Arts of 1925 left their mark upon *Wirt Rowland's* decorative scheme. Everywhere the gaily colored patterns of Pewabic Pottery tiles and rich materials are redolent of the ebullient twenties.

A-3 City-County Building.
Harley, Ellington & Day. 1955.
Jefferson & Woodward. (OP)

Following more or less the general outlines suggested in the *Saarinens'* plan, this combined city hall and county building houses offices, court rooms, and meeting rooms. It consists of two architectural masses, a clever use of black and white marble emphasizing the verticality of the 19-story tower section, markedly contrasting with the 14-story office section. Sculptor Marshall M. Fredericks' bronze Spirit of Detroit fronts the windowless Woodward Ave. facade.

A-4 Mariners P.E. Church.
Calvin N. Otis. 1849.
Jefferson & Randolph. (BHC)

The oldest stone church surviving in Detroit and the town's first stone Gothic Revival church. It was built as a sailors' mission with the bequest of Charlotte Ann Taylor and her sister Mrs. Julia Ann Anderson, and was moved from the N.W. corner of Woodward & Woodbridge (1955); alterations include an added tower.

After the fire of 1805 the Indian Council House was built on the site. It was replaced by Firemen's Hall (1851), actually a social and art exhibition center. Governor Hull's mansion (1807) was across the street, east.

A-5 Henry and Edsel Ford Auditorium.
O'Dell, Hewlett & Luckenbach. 1955.
Civic Center. (BK)

In their plans for the Civic Center, the *Saarinens* indicated an auditorium at the eastern end. Financed by the city, the Ford family, and dealers affiliated with the Ford Motor Co., the architects collaborated with *Crane, Kiehler & Kellogg,* who had had considerable experience in theater construction, including Orchestra Hall and many of Detroit's largest theaters.

The curved front wall and the long walls of the stage enclosure are faced with mica-flecked blue granite to create shimmering effects at night. The side walls are of white marble. Severely plain on the interior, the auditorium seats 2,900.

A-6 Cobo Hall and Convention Arena.
Giffels & Rossetti. 1960.
1 Washington Blvd. (DRI)

The massive rectangular bulk of Cobo Hall defines the western extremity of the Civic Center, and its white marble facade provides a striking contrast to the dark green granite walls of the Convention Arena. An interesting aspect of the design of the complex is the way it is linked to the freeway system. The Lodge Freeway dramatically plunges under Cobo Hall at the precise point where the glass-enclosed administrative offices are cantilevered out over the main entrance.

There are 300,000 square feet of exhibition space and innumerable meeting rooms, as well as a ballroom on the lower level with a large cafeteria above, providing a panoramic view of the Detroit River and Windsor, Canada, to the south.

A-7 T. W. Palmer Block.
Mason & Rice. 1894.
Cass & Larned. (ELA)

Since this was a warehouse, there was no necessity for large windows and the architects sought to emphasize the smooth unbroken surface of the bricks, yet monotony was avoided by devotion to subtle details, such as the gracefully flaring cornice and the molded bricks of the arches and piers.

A-8 Pontchartrain Hotel.
King & Lewis. 1965.
Washington & Jefferson. (BK)

The Ponch, as it is familiarly known, drew its name from Cadillac's *Fort Pontchartrain du Detroit,* built more or less on the same site in 1701. It was the first major hotel to be constructed in Detroit in 38 years. The main floor serves as a base for a glass-walled tower with 450 guest rooms. The glass walls are faceted so that each room has an angular bay commanding simultaneous views of the Detroit River and Canada to the south and the skyline of the city to the north.   27

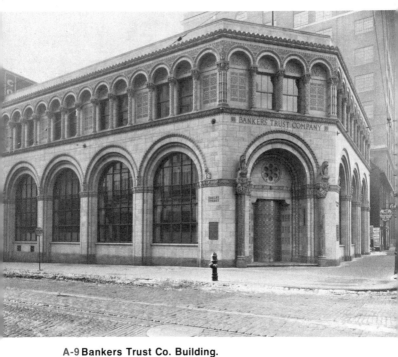

A-9 Bankers Trust Co. Building.
Smith, Hinchman & Grylls. 1925.
Congress & Shelby. (SHG)

Italian Romanesque Revival; designer *Wirt Rowland* used terracotta to imitate stone carving.

A-10 Ford Building.
D. H. Burnham & Co. 1909.
615 Griswold. (MB)

That *Burnham* was affected by the wave of classicism from the East is indicated by a few minor classical details. By and large, however, he followed the Chicago tradition, expressing the steel frame with the clean sharp lines of the white terracotta facing.

A-11 Buhl Building.
Smith, Hinchman & Grylls. 1925.
535 Griswold. (MB)

In general the treatment is Gothic, but the entrance details are Romanesque. An effect of heavy medieval masonry was achieved by the use of random sized terracotta blocks. The abandonment of the classical cornice made possible a stronger vertical emphasis in keeping with the increased height of the building.

A-12 National Bank of Detroit.
Albert Kahn Assoc. 1959.
Woodward & Fort. (BK)

Covering an entire block, it is set back 40 feet from the street to make way for an esplanade shaded by rows of trees, behind which is a covered arcade sheltering the vast glass wall of the 2-story main banking room. Above the arcade stretches the checkered pattern of the curtain wall, enclosing 12 additional stories of office space. Marble was chosen as the material for the infill panels to harmonize with the nearby Civic Center. Numismatists should not overlook the Money Museum on the mezzanine.

    Detroit's first skyscraper, the Hammond Building, *Harry W. J. Edbrooke,* formerly occupied the site. To celebrate its opening in 1890, a tightrope walker was hired to walk across Fort St. from the roof of the 10-story structure to the tower of the 1871 City Hall, *James Anderson* (razed, now Kennedy Sq.).

A-13 National Bank Building.
Albert Kahn Assoc. 1922.
Woodward & Cadillac Sq. (H-B)

Recalling the design of *Kahn's* gigantic General Motors Building of the same year (B-43), monumental classical Corinthian pillars, based on the columns of the Temple of Castor and Pollux in the Roman Forum, rather than Renaissance arcades, dominate the second story.

A-14 Wayne County Building.
John & Arthur Scott. 1902.
Cadillac Sq. & Randolph. (MB)

Cost was apparently not a factor and at the turn of the century
this was unquestionably the most sumptuous building in
Michigan. It remains today an outstanding monument of ''Age
of Elegance'' Roman Baroque. The heroic bronze quadrigas,
symbolizing Progress and flanking the portico, are the work of
sculptor J. Massey Rhind.

West, on Cadillac Sq., are the Cadillac Square Building,
Louis Kamper (1918) and Cadillac (formerly Barlum) Tower,
Bonnah & Chaffee (1927).

A-15 Saints Peter and Paul R.C. Church.
Francis Letourno. 1848.
629 E. Jefferson. (BHC)

The oldest edifice of worship in Detroit. Its walls are broken into bays by Ionic pilasters supporting a classic entablature. The front entrance, centering a projecting bay, is framed by a pediment and Ionic pilasters, and this 3-aisled brick basilica is barrel vaulted in plaster. The architect's original perspective drawing included a Wren-like tower, never constructed.

A-16 Union Railroad Station.
James Stewart & Co. 1893.
Fort & Third. (MB)

A massive clock tower dominates Romanesque arcades and square-headed windows and dormers. The interior has been drastically modernized.

A-17 Fort Street Presbyterian Church.
Octavius & Albert Jordan. 1855.
Fort & Third. (DIA)

Among the welter of archeologically correct early Gothic Revival stone detail it is possible to recognize facsimiles of a corner turret of King's College Chapel, Cambridge, and the slender spire of St. James, Louth, Lincolnshire, England. Despite discrepancies, the church has been much admired for its lacy stonework and graceful silhouette.

A-18 Detroit Bank & Trust Building.
Harley, Ellington, Cowin & Stirton. 1962.
Fort & Washington. (C-C)

The 28-story structure strikes a note of restrained dignity befitting a bank. Dark-tinted floor-to-ceiling windows are set in precast concrete frames which, projecting from the glass, combine into a grid pattern to give the building its essential character. Following recent trends, it is set back from the street to provide for a landscaped plaza.

35

A-19 Detroit Trust Co. Building.
Albert Kahn Assoc. 1915.
Fort & Shelby. (H-B)

Lavish Corinthian columns and pilasters reflect the Italian
Renaissance Revival launched by *McKim, Mead & White* in
New York. It was enlarged in 1926 and the interior was modern-
ized in 1966.

A-20 Peoples State Bank Building.
McKim, Mead & White. 1900.
Fort & Shelby. (HHR)

It is said *Stanford White* took a leading part in designing this
building. Certainly it is not difficult to detect in the exquisite
refinement of its details and proportions the handiwork of the
most gifted and fastidious of the partners. (Manufacturers
National Bank of Detroit.)

A-21 Penobscot Building.
Smith, Hinchman & Grylls. 1928.
645 Griswold. (L-A)

Wirt Rowland was searching for a new idiom for skyscraper design. Its simple limestone mass, H-shaped in plan, rises unbroken to the 30th floor, then a series of setbacks ascend in a masterly cubistic composition to the apex. Dominating the Detroit skyline with its towering bulk (47 stories), the Penobscot Building was a significant achievement.

A-22 Detroit Club.
Wilson Eyre Jr. 1891.
Cass & Fort (BHC)

Belonging to a purely social organization and still in use, it breathes an air of old-fashioned gentility. Alternating round- and flat-headed Renaissance windows characterize an otherwise Richardsonian-Romanesque structure. *Eyre*, a Philadelphian, also designed the Freer House (B-42).

A-23 Federal Reserve Bank Annex.
Smith, Hinchman & Grylls. 1951.
Fort & Shelby. (L-A)

The first important structure erected since the 1920's in downtown Detroit was the 8-story annex to the Detroit Branch of the Federal Reserve Bank of Chicago, *Graham, Anderson, Probst & White* (1927).

To many architects the prospect of building an addition to a 23-year-old bank would have had limited appeal, but to *Minoru Yamasaki,* chief designer at *Smith, Hinchman & Grylls* at the time, it offered interesting possibilities. In contrast to the compact mass of the masonry-backed marble of the original building, the annex is faced with a thin curtain wall of alternating bands of glass and marble veneer, and set back 30 feet from the sidewalk, making room for attractive patches of greenery. By introducing new concepts of design and construction, and by allowing space on the ground level for landscaping, Yamasaki ushered in a new era of commercial architecture in downtown Detroit.

The intersection of Fort and Shelby marks the center of the site of Fort Lernoult/Shelby (1779).

A-24 Dime Building.
D. H. Burnham & Co. 1910.
719 Griswold. (MB)

The wave of classical influence from the East on Chicagoan *Burnham* is more in evidence here than in his Ford Building (A-10) of the previous year. It is U-shaped above the ground floors to afford a light well. 39

A-25 Detroit Cornice & Slate Co.
1897. 733 St. Antoine. (JSC)

The entire front of galvanized steel was manufactured by the company that still occupies this somewhat *retardataire* building.

A-26 Detroit News Building.
Albert Kahn Assoc. 1916.
615 W. Lafayette. (H-B)

With this building *Kahn* established the character of much of his later commercial work. Strictly speaking it is an industrial plant, but its location near the commercial hub of the city and the nature of the newspaper industry demanded it be given a more formal architectural treatment than a factory. George G. Booth, president of the *News* and founder of Cranbrook (I-13), supervised the decoration, which reflects his interest in the Arts and Crafts movement.

A-27 Detroit Free Press Building.
Albert Kahn Assoc. 1923.
321 W. Lafayette. (H-B)

Since the building includes rental space, it is larger than the News Building. Hence, steel construction was preferable to the bulkier reinforced concrete, but the same use of limestone on the exterior was continued. A new element that also differentiates it from the News Building may be noted in the massive 13-story central tower with lower 6-story wings.

41

A-28 Bagley Memorial Fountain.
H. H. Richardson. 1887.
Campus Martius. (BHC)

Fashioned entirely of white granite, this memorial to John J. Bagley, a tobacco magnate and governor of Michigan, 1873-77, is an adaptation of a ciborium in St. Mark's Basilica, Venice. Unless he did the John N. Bagley house (B-5), this is the only surviving structure by *Richardson* in Detroit; his Bagley Memorial Armory on Congress St. was demolished in 1957.

Nearby, at the head of Cadillac Sq., is sculptor Randolph Rogers' Civil War memorial, the Soldiers and Sailors Monument (1872). The site of the first City Hall, *Alpheus White* (1835) is a few yards east.

A-29 First Federal Bank Building.
Smith, Hinchman & Grylls. 1965.
1001 Woodward. (BK)

After prolonged research, the architects were able to make granite an economically feasible material by developing granite-veneered precast window units. The dark color lowered maintenance costs and contrasts with other buildings in the area.

A-30 Sheraton-Cadillac Hotel.
Louis Kamper. 1924.
Washington & Michigan. (BHC)

Unquestionably the most ambitious undertaking of the Book brothers was the mammoth Book-Cadillac Hotel with 1,200 rooms, each with bath. Seconding their notions, *Kamper* indulged his taste for lavish splendor. Today, all is changed. The public has no inclination to be dazzled, and walls and ceilings have been covered with sleek modern surfaces. Even the proud name of Book has disappeared.

A-31 David Stott Building.
Donaldson & Meier. 1929.
1150 Griswold. (MB)

Towering above Capitol Park, a shaft of tan-orange brick rises from a reddish granite base to the 23rd story where it is broken by a series of discreet setbacks. The parapets at each setback are ornamented with terracotta, graduated in tone from deep tan at the lowest level to buff at the top.

Perhaps more than any other man, it was *Eliel Saarinen* who gave the skyscraper a definitive form; although his Chicago Tribune Tower project was never realized, its influence is apparent in the design of this building and scores of others across the nation.

A-32 Parker Block.
Gordon W. Lloyd. 1883.
1075 Woodward. (ELA)

A rare surviving example of the once prevalent overdecorated cast-iron front retail-store building of the Victorian era. (B. Siegel Co.)

A-33 Chamber of Commerce Building.
Spier & Rohns. 1895.
Griswold & State. (BHC)

One of the first metal-skeleton skyscrapers built in Detroit. Outside and inside walls and floors are supported on the iron frame. The rusticated base, arcades, pillars, and flaring cornices of Italian Renaissance palaces were adapted to a larger commercial structure. It faces Capitol Park, site of Michigan's first capitol, *Obed Wait* (1828).

A-34 D. M. Ferry & Co. Warehouse.
Gordon W. Lloyd. 1887.
Brush & Lafayette. (GDM)

In the formalization of the brick exterior, *Lloyd* was undoubtedly influenced by *Richardson's* Marshall Field Wholesale Warehouse in Chicago, but made no attempt to emulate its sublety of proportions. Although seed merchant Dexter M. Ferry's previous building on the site, *Mason & Rice* (1881), was equipped with new-fangled automatic sprinklers, on 1 Jan. 1886 it was demolished in one of Detroit's most spectacular fires, made pungent with the odor of smouldering seeds.

A-35 Michigan Blue Cross/Blue Shield Service Center.
Giffels & Rossetti (Louis A. Rossetti). 1971.
Lafayette & St. Antoine. (LA)

The center includes a 22-story office tower, a 3-story support facility, and a 5-level parking structure for 1,262 cars. They surround a multi-level landscaped plaza, furnishing employees and the general public a relaxing environment.

Holy Family R. C. Church, *Van Leyen & Schilling* (1910), 641 Chrysler (Hastings), will continue to occupy a portion of the site.

A-36 Dowling Hall, University of Detroit.
Gordon W. Lloyd. 1891.
651 E. Jefferson. (MB)

Richardson-Romanesque Revival Collegiate, originally Detroit College (Jesuit).   47

A-37 St. Mary R. C. Church.
Peter Dederichs. 1885.
St. Antoine & Monroe. (JSC)

From the Pisan Romanesque and Venetian Renaissance *Dederichs* extracted diverse details and ingeniously fused them into a composite fabric of great originality.

A-38 St. Mary R. C. Rectory.
Julius Hess. 1876.
646 Monroe. (JSC)

An example of North Italian "banded" Romanesque, made popular by the writings of John Ruskin.

A-39 Book Building and Book Tower.
Louis Kamper. 1917, 1926.
Washington & Grand River. (MB)

The first product of the collaboration of *Kamper* and the brothers Herbert, Frank, and J. Burgess Book, Jr. (C-7) to beautify Washington Blvd. was the Book Building, a handsome, stone-faced, 13-story structure with Italianate details. A curious feature is a series of 12 nude caryatids supporting the cornice.

Kamper unsuccessfully tried to relieve the vast expanse of wall surface of the 36-story Book Tower with horizontal bands of Italian Renaissance ornamentation, greatly enlarged so as to be visible. He failed to realize the effectiveness of the design of a skyscraper lies more in its mass than in its detail.

A-40 Detroit Police Headquarters.
Albert Kahn Assoc. 1923.
Beaubien & Macomb. (H-B)

By borrowing from Italian palaces, *Kahn* was able to give the building an appearance suggesting order and authority.

A-41 T. B. Rayl Co. Building.
Baxter, O'Dell & Halpin. 1915.
Woodward & Grand River. (MB)

The red terracotta facing with rich surface ornament, slender piers terminating in arcades, and cavetto cornice exemplify the influence of the genius of *Louis H. Sullivan.*

A-42 Woodward Building.
Albert Kahn Assoc. 1915.
Woodward & Clifford. (MB)

Kahn's white terracotta piers and iron spandrels for bold arches show the influence of *Sullivan's* restrained, delicate detail.

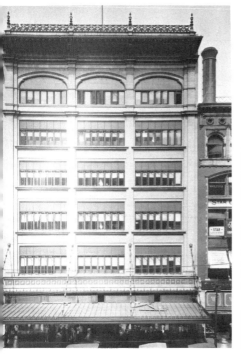 

A-43 D. J. Healy Co. Building.
Postle & Mahler. 1910.
1426 Woodward. (MB)

Although the building is Sullivanian in its general aspect and was designed by a Chicago firm, the cornice and friezes are Renaissance in character.

A-44 David Whitney Building.
D. H. Burnham & Co. 1915.
Park & Woodward. (MB)

Corridors face an inside court, permitting outside exposure for all offices. The Italian Renaissance provided motifs for the exterior ornament. This increasingly archeological detail was an indication of the decline of the impact of the Chicago School in Detroit.

A-45 Detroit Athletic Club.
Albert Kahn Assoc. 1915.
251 Madison. (H-B)

Inspired by Renaissance Roman palaces, *Kahn* derived most of the fenestration from the piazza facade of the Palazzo Farnese, with its arcaded loggia court furnishing the design for the windows of the fourth floor dining room.

A-46 Detroit-Hilton Hotel.
George B. Post. 1914.
Park & Washington. (BHC)

Subtle Italian Renaissance details with strong Adam influence give this 18-story hotel a luxurious atmosphere and set a new standard of excellence for hotels in Detroit. (Originally, Statler Hotel.)

A-47 R. H. Fyfe's Shoe Store Building.
Smith, Hinchman & Grylls. 1919.
Adams & Woodward. (BHC)

This handsome example of Gothic commercial architecture with soaring vertical lines and deep window reveals stands as a landmark at the head of the busy thoroughfares that converge on Grand Circus Park. In 1962 the floors above the third level were converted into apartments.

A-48 Central Methodist Church.
Gordon W. Lloyd. 1867.
Woodward & Adams. (DIA)

Restrained ornamentation and rugged masonry characterize
this Gothic Revival church with broad, semi-octagonal transepts
and large gables.

A-49 St. John P. E. Church.
Jordan & Anderson. 1861.
Woodward & Vernor (Fisher Fwy.). (DIA)

There was no need for economizing as Henry P. Baldwin, a shoe manufacturer, unstintingly provided the funds for the construction of this limestone church with cut stone trimmings. Here we recognize the earmarks of Victorian Gothic at its best.

B.

East Warren

Van Dyke

East Grand Boulevard

Mt. Elliott

Gratiot

12
7

11

2-a

Jefferson

10
9 8

6 5

2 3 4

N

B-1 Ste. Anne R. C. Church.
Leon Coquard. 1887.
Howard & St. Anne (19th). (C-C)

Ste. Anne's is the oldest parish in Detroit and this is the 8th structure (the first was built in 1701 in Cadillac's fort). In the crypt lie the remains of Father Gabriel Richard and in the chapel are relics from the church he built downtown in 1828. William Woolfenden has pointed out that, cruciform in plan, it follows twin-towered French prototypes rather than English, as did the majority of Gothic Revival churches.

B-2 Christ P. E. Church.
Gordon W. Lloyd. 1863.
960 E. Jefferson. (MB)

Its massive and distinctive Gothic belfry dominates the debouchment of Chrysler Freeway onto Jefferson Ave.

B-3 Sibley House.
1848. 976 E. Jefferson. (HAL)

The widow of Judge Solomon Sibley built this frame house for herself and her two daughters. It is one of the few surviving early 19th century residences in Detroit.

B-4 Trowbridge House.
1826. 1380 E. Jefferson. (JPM)

When Charles C. Trowbridge, cashier and later president of the Bank of Michigan, built his frame house it was considered the finest in the territory. In later years it was considerably altered and reduced in size.

B-5 John N. Bagley House.
1889. Jefferson & Joseph Campau. (JSC)

Red brick Romanesque Revival with brownstone trim carved by Julius T. Melchers. Since *H. H. Richardson* designed a fountain (A-28) and an armory for the Bagleys, he also may have furnished plans for a residence, but there is no known documentary evidence.

B-6 Alexander Chene House.
c. 1850. 2681 E. Jefferson. (JPM)

The finest surviving old "Federal Style" house in Detroit. (Little Harry's Restaurant.)

B-7 Elmwood Park North.
Eberle M. Smith Assoc. 1966.
Antietam & St. Aubin. (BK)

Elmwood Park, a 500-acre downtown redevelopment project *(Crane & Gorwic),* will eventually accommodate 15,000 people. The success of the town houses in Lafayette Park led to the decision to build mainly low-rise units in the new project. However, 3 high-rise apartments will be located in a central 22-acre park, around which will be grouped several medium-rise apartments. Elmwood Park Drive, a winding boulevard, will be the only through route in the project. Town houses will be reached by service drives at the rear, and landscaped walkways will lead from the fronts of the houses to the park.

Lafayette Park

For many years the area directly east of downtown had been steadily declining. After World War II it became apparent that the only hope for the area was redevelopment. In 1946 plans were formulated for the clearance of 129 acres of slums bounded by Gratiot, Dequindre, Hastings, and Lafayette, and funds were appropriated by the city for land acquisition. The passage of the National Housing Act of 1949 gave assurance of federal assistance. By the end of 1954 the land was cleared. From the beginning the Housing Commission intended the project to be open to private developers, but it was no easy task to reverse the trend to the suburbs and at first builders shied away from such an unconventional venture.

Finally a group of citizens representing business, industry, and labor stepped into the vacuum left by public apathy. Organized as the Citizens Redevelopment Corp., it attempted to promote the development of the Gratiot area. Concluding that to lure suburbanites back to the city it was necessary to create a unique project, it engaged *Oscar Stonorov, Victor Gruen & Assoc.,* and *Leinweber, Yamasaki & Hellmuth* to produce a plan. They developed a scheme of high-rise apartments and low-rise housing with open spaces intervening.

B-8 1300 Lafayette East.
Birkerts & Straub. 1964.
Lafayette & Rivard. (BK)

A 30-story apartment building, its elegance lies in its tapering thinness. Wall surfaces are composed of precast window bays and tapering reinforced concrete columns spaced to correspond with differing room widths. The two halves of the building are offset, emphasizing even more the effect of thinness.

B-9 Lafayette Park Pavilion Apartments.
Ludwig Mies van der Rohe. 1959.
1 Lafayette Plaisance. (H-B)

The 22-story Pavilion Apartments exemplify the serene and classic discipline of the architect. Framed in concrete, they are faced with aluminum and gray glass. Around cul-de-sacs are grouped 186 low-rise apartments. These include 2-story town houses and 1-story court houses. Glass window walls and yellow brick end walls are framed by the black outlines of exposed structural steel. Brick-walled courts adjoining the 1-story units provide private outdoor living areas, and informal planting softens the architectural lines.

B-10 Lafayette Park Regency Square.
Green & Savin. 1966.
1941 Orleans. (B-K)

B-11 Church of the Messiah.
Calvin N. Otis. 1852.
Grand Blvd. & Lafayette. (BHC)

Basically a New England meetinghouse, the only change being the substitution of Gothic for Georgian motifs. Originally St. Paul P. E. Church, and eventually outgrown, in 1901 the church was moved, stone by stone, from downtown to its present site and lost its spire.

B-12 St. Joseph R. C. Church.
Francis G. Himpler. 1873.
Jay & Orleans. (JSC)

The tall windows, steep roof, and soaring frontal tower recall the *Hallenkirchen* of southern Germany. It was the last in the cycle of Detroit's native limestone churches.

B-13 Woodward Avenue Baptist Church.
Mortimer L. Smith. 1887.
Woodward & Winder. (BHC)

Later Victorian Gothic with fussy exterior detail, but with a magnificent interior of iron columns, trusses, and galleries on 4 sides.

B-14 Ransom Gillis House.
Brush & Mason. 1876.
Alfred & John R. (MB)

Replete with the north Italian turrets, gables, leaf-capital colonettes, and banded arches beloved by Ruskin.

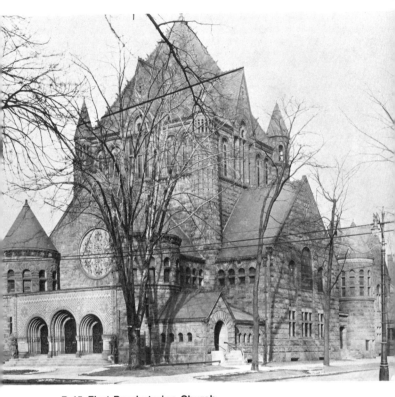

B-15 First Presbyterian Church.
Mason & Rice. 1889.
Woodward & Edmund Pl. (MB)

As in *Richardson's* Trinity Church, enormous masonry arches support a massive tower, but there are certain marked differences from the Boston masterpiece: rock-faced red sandstone instead of granite, less archeological details, general outline much more compact. The plan is actually a Greek cross and there is an intimacy altogether lacking in Trinity. When Woodward was widened in 1936, the handsome triple-arched entrance porch with its charming marquetry and stone carving was shifted from the western to the southern facade.

B-16 Church of Christ.
Donaldson & Meier. 1890.
Woodward & Edmund Pl. (MB)

Originally, First Unitarian Church; altered.

B-17 Masonic Temple.
George D. Mason & Co. 1928.
500 Temple (Cass Park). (BHC)

"The spirit and tradition of the Knights Templars was unquestionably Romanesque or Gothic," said architect *Mason,* "and operative Masonry, having its origin in the guilds of Europe, had the tradition of the great cathedrals, of which Masons were the builders."

69

B-18 Trinity P. E. Church.
Mason & Rice. 1892.
Myrtle & Trumbull (JSC)

Newspaper publisher James E. Scripps built this late 14th century southern English Gothic church near his own neo-Tudor residence (B-21) at his own expense, to "stimulate, if possible, in church architecture, a return to the older and more truly artistic forms."

B-19 Medical Center Professional Plaza.
Crane & Gorwic. 1966.
3800 Woodward. (C-C)

Elevators, stairwells, and washrooms are grouped at the center, thus eliminating long corridors and providing outside exposure for offices in this 15-story tower. Floor space is clear of columns, which were placed inside the utility core or projected out from the tinted thermal glass of the curtain walls.

Across Woodward at Parsons is *C. Howard Crane's* Orchestra Hall (1919).

B-20 Temple Beth El.
Mason & Kahn. 1903.
3424 Woodward. (AKA)

Obviously derived from the domed and porticoed Roman
Pantheon, but *Albert Kahn* finished it with Louis XVI decoration.
Altered and defaced after the congregation moved to a new
Kahn temple far out Woodward (1922), it is now the Bonstelle
Theatre of Wayne State University.

B-21 James E. Scripps House.
Mason & Rice. 1891.
3664 Trumbull. (JSC)

This soaring English baronial castle with crenelated walls, dominated by an octagonal tower, belonged to George G. Booth's father-in-law. The adjoining Gothic library and art gallery, modeled after the chapter house at Westminster Abbey, *Nettleton & Kahn* (1898), has been razed. (The art collection was given to the Detroit Institute of Arts.) Booth's own pre-Cranbrook (I-13) Dutch Renaissance house, also by *Mason & Rice* (1889), and across the street, has been razed too.

B-22 Cass Avenue Methodist Church.
Malcomson & Higginbotham. 1891.
Cass & Selden. (JSC)

One of several Romanesque Revival churches designed by this firm in the 1890's (another is on Woodward at Ford Freeway), whose towers suggest medieval fortresses.

Medical Center

After World War II the area north of the downtown district was a no man's land of dilapidated industrial, commercial, and residential buildings. Among them stood 4 of Detroit's most venerated medical institutions: Children's, Hutzel, Grace, and Harper Hospitals. Without some positive action, it was only a matter of time before they would be engulfed by the blight surrounding them.

Then Wayne State University School of Medicine proposed affiliation with these institutions to form a great center for medical education. In 1955 the hospitals and the School of Medicine organized the Detroit Medical Center Citizens Committee to create a complex that would utilize the existing hospitals as a core around which to develop other facilities for medical care, teaching, and research. The committee engaged the services of *Gerald Crane,* whose master plan for the Medical Center was published in 1958. In 1961 *Crane* joined with *Norbert Gorwic* to form the firm of *Crane & Gorwic Assoc.,* who published a revised master plan in 1966, which embodies several objectives: blocks assembled into superblocks for best use of available land, separated vehicular and pedestrian traffic, reorganized street system, expansion of existing institutions.

A medical core of 100 acres devoted entirely to medical care, teaching, and research will contain the existing hospitals and the Wayne State University School of Medicine. A landscaped walkway, extending the full length of the core, will replace Brush St.; vehicular access to the core will be accomplished by an internal ring road; around the core will be a wide belt devoted entirely to residential, commercial, and related uses; and parking will be accommodated in above ground and underground structures, and on surface lots.

B-23 Children's Hospital of Michigan.
Albert Kahn Assoc. 1971.
Medical Center. (FS)

Facing materials are exposed concrete, brick, and aluminum and glass panels. A 3-story "H" containing all patient rooms is atop a 3-story square housing all other facilities.

B-24 Medical Research Building, W.S.U.
Smith, Hinchman & Grylls. 1964.
Medical Center. (SHG)

Research areas are grouped around a central longitudinal utility core containing mechanical and electrical services. A grille of buff-colored precast concrete serves as a curtain wall and provides daylight for the peripheral corridors to the laboratories.

B-25 Webber Memorial Building,
Harper-Grace Hospital.
Smith, Hinchman & Grylls, 1977.
John R & Alexandrine. (BK)

Harper-Grace Hospital is a 999-bed adult clinical teaching and research affiliate of the Wayne State University School of Medicine.

In the complex, the new Webber Memorial Building's 670 beds, 22 operating rooms, 21 diagnostic X-ray rooms, nuclear medicine laboratories, and 28 specialized laboratories are combined with the remodeled Hudson and Brush Buildings. A new parking structure provides 1,000 parking spaces. McLaughlin Hall was remodeled into an out-patient clinic, and Grace Memorial Building is being remodeled and expanded.

B-26 David Whitney Jr. House.
Gordon W. Lloyd. 1894.
4421 Woodward. (MB)

Acclaimed when built as "the most pretentious modern home
in the state and one of the most elaborate houses in the West."
The facing is jasper. (Visiting Nurse Association.)

B-27 Vera Parshall Shiffman Medical Library, W.S.U.
O'Dell, Hewlett & Luckenbach. 1970.
Medical Center. (BK)

This relatively small building attains dominance in the center from its sculptured facade of smooth and ribbed limestone and from its placement on an earth berm podium supported by concrete pilotis. It has some of the most sophisticated suspended stone detailing to be built this century in the Detroit area.

B-28 Sweetest Heart of Mary R. C. Church.
Spier & Rohns. 1893.
Russell & Canfield. (JSC)

The twin-towered Gothic of northern Europe was not ignored by Detroit church builders. The brick exterior displays a multiplicity of forms.

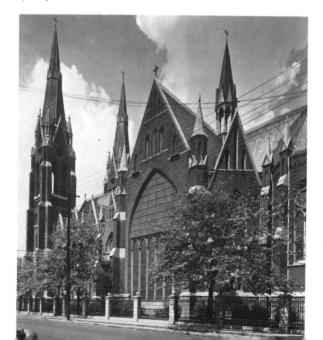

77

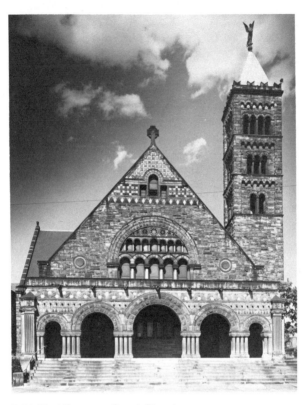

B-29 First Congregational Church.
J. Lyman Faxon. 1891.
Woodward & Forest. (JSC)

An adept blending of elements drawn from the Romanesque and Byzantine of Italy and Dalmatia with an especially handsome campanile.

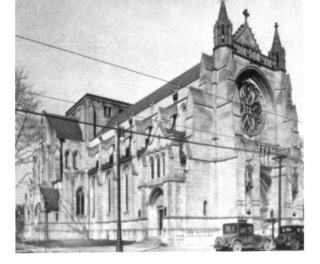

B-30 St. Paul P. E. Cathedral.
Cram, Goodhue & Ferguson. 1911.
Woodward & Hancock. (MB)

With graceful rose and lancet windows, and jutting buttresses heralding the influence of 14th and 15th century English Gothic, this monumental edifice would overpower Woodward Ave. to a greater extent had the planned soaring crossing tower been built.

B-31 Maccabees Building.
Albert Kahn Assoc. 1927.
Woodward & Putnam. (H-B)

No doubt influenced by *Walker's* New York Telephone Building, this 14-story tower with subordinate masses flanking open courts creates an imposing 3-dimensional composition.

Cultural Center

The nucleus of the Detroit Cultural Center was established early in this century. With considerable foresight, civic leaders purchased ideal sites for the future Detroit Public Library and Detroit Institute of Arts to complement one another across Woodward Ave., about two miles north of the downtown business district. Even in the early plans related buildings were to be clustered around the library and the art museum, two of which were specifically referred to as "school of design," and "hall for music." Dedicated in 1921, the Public Library set a new standard of magnificence for Detroit; six years later, the Institute of Arts was opened, rivaling its sister institution in its white marble splendor. Architecturally, they are outstanding examples of public buildings in the academic style.

The Cultural Center area remained unchanged from the completion of the Institute of Arts in 1927 until 1941, when the Horace H. Rackham Educational Memorial, *Harley, Ellington & Day,* was built directly south of the art museum.

With the establishment of a master plan for Detroit in 1941, a new era in city planning was inaugurated. In 1945 *Buford L. Pickens* of Wayne University was engaged by the City Plan Commission to prepare plans for the future expansion of the Cultural Center. In the area east of the Institute of Arts he envisioned a museum of industry, historical, natural science, and social science museums, and a planetarium and astronomical institute. Included in the plan were suggestions for an adjoining medical science center to the east and an expanded Wayne University campus to the west.

Studies for the Cultural Center were continued by *Suren Pilafian,* who had won the competition for a Wayne University campus plan in 1942. His designs were incorporated in a 1948 brochure entitled *Cultural Center Plan.* Since then, many buildings or additions proposed in the brochure have become reality.

The City Plan Commission came forward in 1965 with a new plan more comprehensive in scope than any previous plan. To create an atmosphere of repose and to facilitate pedestrian circulation, the Cultural Center is to be divided into three islands: Wayne State University, Detroit Public Library, and Cultural Center Park. Institutions to be grouped around a reflecting pool in a landscaped setting will include a hall of man, planetarium, museum of science and technology, centers for musical and theater arts, and the existing Institute of Arts.

B-32 Life Sciences Research Center.
Albert Kahn Assoc. 1960.
W.S.U. Mall (Second) & Warren. (BK)

Tall narrow windows are divided by projecting columns of poured concrete which double as sun baffles; wall panels of quartz aggregate provide textural richness; a recessed arcade on the ground level enhances the visual appeal; and a graceful crown of precast concrete conceals mechanical equipment.

B-33 Old Main, W.S.U.
Malcomson & Higginbotham. 1896.
Cass & Hancock. (WSU)

Built as Central High School. Postgraduate courses evolved into a municipal university which took over the entire building and overflowed up Cass and Second Aves., inaugurating a massive building program, still in progress. Wayne became a state university in 1956, and dates its founding from that of its School of Medicine (1868).

81

B-34 Detroit Public Library.
Cass Gilbert. 1921.
North and South Wings.
Francis J. Keally and *Cass Gilbert Jr.* 1963.
5201 Woodward. (CHE)

The lines of the central building were continued in the wings in a simplified version of the original Italian Renaissance style by the son of its architect. The same Vermont marble was used throughout with the addition of serpentine Italian marble trim. The Burton Historical Collection is housed in the North Wing, and the Detroit Historical Museum, *William E. Kapp* (1951), is across the street, north.

B-35 Kresge Science Library.
Pilafian & Montana. 1953.
W.S.U. Mall near Kirby. (H B)

With sweeping horizontal lines and cantilevered upper stories, this is one of *Pilafian's* most successful buildings.

B-36 Meyer and Anna Prentis Building, W.S.U.
Minoru Yamasaki & Assoc. 1964.
Cass near Kirby. (WSU)

Precast concrete wall panels were used in this School of Business Administration building. There is a clear differentiation between ground floor arcade and upper stories, fenestration is arranged in neat horizontal tiers, and a certain elegance of proportion is enhanced by delicately tapering columns.

B-37 Detroit Institute of Arts.
Paul P. Cret and *Zantzinger, Borie & Medary.* 1927.
South (Farnsworth) and North (Kirby) Wings.
Harley, Ellington, Cowin & Stirton and
Gunnar Birkerts & Assoc. 1966, 1971.
5200 Woodward. (JKJ)

It would have been prohibitively costly to duplicate the white marble moldings and carvings of the Italian Renaissance central building, so the architects of the new wings wisely decided to provide contrast by giving them a decidedly contemporary treatment. The unbroken dark gray granite walls do not compete with the old building, but serve rather as backgrounds to emphasize its fine details. Nowhere is the contrast between old and new more dramatic than in the twin 3-story courts where jutting modern balconies provide foils for the exquisitely detailed marble walls of the central building.

B-38 McGregor Memorial Conference Center.
Minoru Yamasaki & Assoc. 1958.
Ferry & W.S.U. Mall. (H-B)

End walls are of travertine marble. On the inside there are rows of conference rooms divided by a 2-story lounge and reception area at the center. The triangular ends of the V-shaped ceiling beams are exposed inside and out, and form the basis of a decorative pattern repeated with variations throughout the building. Above the lounge is a skylight composed of glass pyramids, and at each end is a glass cage penetrated by cast aluminum doors. Everywhere the richness of the materials used is apparent — in the white marble columns and floors, in the teak-wood doors, in the black leather Barcelona chairs, and in turkey-red carpeting.

B-39 Shapero Hall of Pharmacy.
Paulsen & Gardner. 1965.
W.S.U. Mall & Ferry. (BK)

In this inverted stepped pyramid of concrete, laboratories, which need the most space and the most isolation, are in the upper stories, while activities involving the most traffic are centered in the 2-story base, which includes a lobby and lecture hall. A low building was to have encircled the main building in a second phase of construction.

B-40 Woodward Elementary School.
Meathe, Kessler & Assoc. 1963.
2900 Wreford. (BK)

Economy of plan and materials were primary considerations in the construction of this square box with gymnasium and auditorium in the center. A recessed first floor averts a boxy look, precast concrete panels on the second floor contrast with dark brick on the first floor, and concrete "eyebrows" and T-shaped columns add interest.

B-41 Frank J. Hecker House.
Scott, Kamper & Scott, 1890.
Woodward & Ferry. (ELA)

Inspired by the Chateau de Chenonceaux near Tours. The beautifully carved stone detailing struck a new note of sophistication in the gay nineties. (Smiley Bros. Music Co.)

B-42 Charles Lang Freer House.
Wilson Eyre Jr. 1890.
71 E. Ferry. (ELA)

According to Wayne Andrews, the finest example in Michigan of the "Shingle Style," and one of the most distinguished houses of its period in Detroit. It once housed Whistler's famous "Peacock Room," now in Washington, D.C. (Administration Building, Merrill-Palmer Institute.)
   Nearby at 245 E. Kirby is *Yamasaki's* Society of Arts & Crafts School (1958).

B-43 General Motors Building.
Albert Kahn Assoc. 1922.
Grand Blvd. at Cass. (AKA)

There is a distinct relationship, despite archeological details, between the General Motors Building and *Kahn's* industrial work. It, too, was an enormous project of great complexity, carefully organized and unified. The chief architectural interest of the building lies in the masterly handling of units of majestic size.

B-44 Ford Motor Co. (former).
Field, Hinchman & Smith. 1904.
Piquette & Beaubien. (FMC)

A traditional mill building of the type still being built after *Kahn* made industrial architectural history with a reinforced concrete building for the Packard Motor Car Co. on E. Grand Blvd. Ever since 1889 Ford had been struggling to establish himself as a manufacturer of automobiles, but the erection of this factory, ten times the size of his leased building, left no doubt that he was well on the way to success.

B-45 Fisher Building.
Albert Kahn Assoc. 1928.
Grand Blvd. at Second. (H-B)

Kahn's greatest opportunity in commercial architecture came when he was commissioned to design the Fisher Building. It was to be the first and largest of 3 units of a vast "New Center" shopping and office complex planned by the 7 Fisher brothers to provide a secondary business district that would relieve downtown congestion and be more accessible to the suburbs.

The aesthetic aspects of such an important commission required considerable study. *Kahn* was alarmed about the trend of architecture in the ebullient 1920's. In his opinion, Le Corbusier, Gropius, and Mendelsohn had gone too far in the glorification of steel and glass. He recognized that the modern skyscraper deserved an exterior treatment expressive of its structure, but he was wary of indulging in the strange or the bizarre.

The New York Life Insurance Co. Building was probably the prototype, but *Gilbert's* fussy Gothic details were abandoned in favor of a more modern decorative treatment. The Fisher Building is basically L-shaped in plan with a 26-story tower at the angle. Shop windows facing the streets are framed with round arches, and a magnificent 3-story marble-walled interior arcade, giving access to the shops from the rear, extends from one end of the building to the other.

C. East Side and Grosse Pointe

Belle Isle

In the latter half of the 19th century great urban parks and residential avenues were introduced in American cities to compensate for chaotic industrialization and haphazard growth. Many Americans saw and admired the magnificent pleasure areas and boulevards Haussmann had created in Paris for Napoleon III, which set an example for American cities. As Detroit grew larger it became apparent that small parks scattered around the city did not provide adequate breathing space for the populace. Belle Isle in the Detroit River, already being invaded by picknickers disgorged by the increasing number of steamers on the river, seemed a logical place for a large recreational center.

In 1879, at the request of the city council, the legislature in Lansing passed bills providing for the construction of Grand Boulevard and the purchase as a public park of Belle Isle, a wilderness of forest and marsh. The park commissioners promptly called upon the distinguished landscape architect Frederick Law Olmsted to improve and beautify Belle Isle. Michael J. Dee, a newspaperman, conceived the idea of a series of canals covering the island, the earth taken from them to be used to fill in the sloughs and marshes which Olmsted had intended to fill with city refuse. The commissioners were so favorably impressed by Dee's plans that they discarded Olmsted's, retaining only his concept of a central driveway. *John M. Donaldson* was commissioned to bring the work to completion. In 1889 the western end of Belle Isle was connected by a bridge to the eastern end of Grand Boulevard. Through land reclamation the island was increased from 768 to 985 acres by 1941.

One of the most attractive early buildings on Belle Isle is a small police station designed by *Mason & Rice*. The rustic charm of its rough fieldstone and shingled surfaces, suggesting a Norman farmhouse, made it perfectly suited to the naturalistic setting. Its continuous use as a police station is silent testimony

C-1 Belle Isle Police Station.
Mason & Rice. 1893.
Belle Isle. (JSC)

92

of its architectural merit. The Detroit Boat Club, located near the bridge, is the oldest river-club in the United States. Twice destroyed by fire, the present fireproof clubhouse was designed by *Alpheus Chittenden* (1901). *Albert Kahn* was the architect of the Conservatory (1903) and Casino (1908).

In 1900 a Bicentennial Memorial was planned on land reclaimed from the river at the lower end of Belle Isle Park. According to the design commissioned from *Stanford White,* a Doric column, 24 feet in diameter and surrounded by groups of sculpture in the water, was to rise 220 feet, all situated in a court formed by a marble colonnade 1,500 feet long, adorned with statues of Cadillac and others notable in the history of Detroit. On the land behind the colonnade there was to be an artificial lake fed by decorative fountains and faced on either side by an aquarium and a horticultural building. A campaign to raise a million dollars for the monument was launched but somehow failed to capture the imagination of the public sufficiently to make it feasible and it seemed, at least for a while, as if the scheme for the artistic treatment of the foot of Belle Isle was destined for oblivion. But then the unexpected happened. Detroiters, who had envisioned an impressive memorial to honor their city's great, winced when they heard that in its place a monument would be erected in memory of James Scott, a man who had the reputation for being a vindictive scurrilous misanthrope.

During a long life Scott had made shrewd investments in downtown real estate. His enemies were legion, for he delighted in feuds, law suits, and practical jokes. The greatest practical joke of all came at the end of his life, for his will provided that his fortune was to be used to erect a memorial on Belle Isle, to be called the James Scott Fountain. Pulpits thundered in protest against perpetuating the memory of such a man, but the cause of civic beautification won in the end. The fountain was completed 15 years after the death of the donor.

C-2 James Scott Fountain.
Cass Gilbert. 1925.
Belle Isle. (BHC)

Indian Village

The early developers of Indian Village in the 1890's envisioned the area as a community of fine homes with gracious sweeping lawns and lovely gardens. Building continued through the early years of the century and most of the houses in the southern end were built between 1910 and 1920. Many residents of Indian Village were among Detroit's leading citizens.

The wealthy roaring twenties saw some exodus to more elaborate houses, and the depression years that followed brought problems on how to maintain the character, beauty, and dignity of the village. In 1937 the Indian Village Association was formed to cope with zoning violations and to enlist the cooperation of city authorities to preserve the original character of the neighborhood.

C-3 Julius T. Melchers House.
Donaldson & Meier. 1897.
723 Seyburn. (HHR)

J. Gari Melchers, perhaps Detroit's most famous and successful artist, commissioned and gave this Colonial Revival house to his father, Detroit's most beloved and renowned early sculptor, who himself carved the elaborate gable of the central dormer.

C-4 James Hamilton House.
Stratton & Baldwin. 1902.
Jefferson & Parker. (DIA)

A half-timbered house more in the style of Norman Shaw's revival than of Tudor England.

C-5 Jefferson Avenue Presbyterian Church.
Smith, Hinchman & Grylls. 1925.
Jefferson & Burns. (DIA)

Gothic and Medieval motifs are employed with considerable freedom to create picturesque masses of rugged masonry with exaggerated deep reveals.

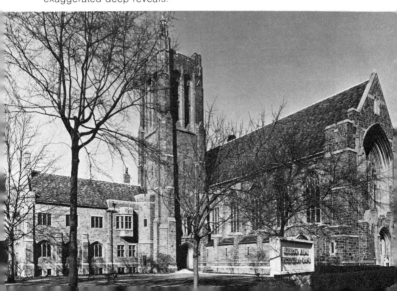

C-6 Dr. Burt Shurly House.
Walter MacFarlane. 1898.
1027 Seminole. (BP)

A typical Indian Village clapboard house, once embellished with a double-deck porch across the entire facade. The interior staircase is a full 360 degrees with a double crystal chandelier hanging in the well.

C-7 James Burgess Book Jr. House.
Louis Kamper. 1911.
Jefferson & Burns. (AS)

Following the tradition of 16th century Italian palaces, balustraded steps lead to a handsome arched entrance flanked by engaged Corinthian columns. The interior is notable for its exquisitely carved marble mantels, marble floors, and ornately molded plaster walls and ceilings.

C-8 Jeffersonian Apartments.
Giffels & Rossetti. 1965.
9000 E. Jefferson. (L-A)

One of the new luxury apartment buildings that are changing the pattern of urban living. Apartment dwellers are offered tall, clean slabs in park-like surroundings with balconies, swimming pools, and other amenities as added attractions. The 30-story Jeffersonian overlooks the Detroit River.

C-9 Hurlbut Memorial Gate.
Brede & Mueller. 1894.
Waterworks Park. (BHC)

C-10 Hannan Memorial YMCA.
Robert O. Derrick. 1927.
10401 E. Jefferson. (HAL)

C-11 Louis Kamper House.
Louis Kamper. c. 1910.
2150 Iroquois. (AS)

Kamper skillfully employed Italian Renaissance columns and superimposed pilasters on the facade of his own house.

C-12 Pewabic Pottery Co.
Stratton & Baldwin. 1907.
10125 E. Jefferson. (DIA)

The "English Cottage" style well suited the image of the semi-handicraft nature of the industry run by Mary Chase Perry Stratton, wife of one of the architects.

Grosse Pointe

Around 1850 Detroiters discovered the sleepy rural community of Grosse Pointe on the shores of Lake St. Clair. Recognizing its recreational advantages, wealthy businessmen bought up old French ribbon farms stretching back from the lake and built summer cottages. At that time there was no easy way to reach Grosse Pointe; the dirt road from the city was impassable for horse and buggy in wet weather. By the 1880's a trolley route was extended to Grosse Pointe along Jefferson Ave., which was paved in 1903 from the Waterworks in Detroit to Fisher Rd. in Grosse Pointe. Summer houses were turned into year-round residences and the community became increasingly elegant. But it remained principally a summer colony until after World War I, when the automobile made it readily accessible. This was all that was needed to convert the summer resort into a thriving suburb.

The prosperity of the twenties manifested itself in Grosse Pointe not only in great mansions, but also in many houses of more modest proportions, which displayed fine workmanship and competent design.

C-13 William B. Stratton House.
William B. Stratton. 1927.
938 Three Mile Dr., Grosse Pointe Park. (DIA)

Stratton and his wife Mary Chase Perry, a founder of Pewabic Pottery (C-12), together worked out many details. Their travels to Mexico and Spain inspired the Spanish atmosphere permeating the house.

C-14 Millard Pryor House.
Alden B. Dow Assoc. 1938.
888 Pemberton, Grosse Pointe Park. (WHF)

This cinder-block structure is unusual for *Dow* in that it leans toward the so-called International Style in its box-like quality and uncompromisingly white exterior. In the 2-story living room, space extends upward to the balcony and outward into the 1-story dining room. A long horizontal pergola ties the house to the site.

C-15 William H. Kessler House.
Meathe, Kessler & Assoc. 1959.
1013 Cadieux, Grosse Pointe Park. (BK)

C-16 John M. Dwyer House.
Raymond Carey. 1909.
370 Lakeland, Grosse Pointe. (HAL)

Noteworthy for its semi-circular colonnaded porch and handsome pediment above the central bay.

C-17 Charles M. Swift House.
Albert Kahn Assoc. 1905.
17840 Jefferson, Grosse Pointe. (AKA)

One of *Kahn's* earliest Tudor houses, it is faced in random gray
ashlar and stands on a point overlooking Lake St. Clair.

C-18 Grosse Pointe Public Library.
Marcel Breuer. 1953.
10 Kercheval, Grosse Pointe Farms. (SP)

C-19 Russell A. Alger House.
Charles A. Platt. 1910.
32 Lake Shore, Grosse Pointe Farms. (HHR)

The beauty of this Italian Renaissance villa may now be enjoyed by the community as a whole, for it is now the Grosse Pointe War Memorial, a community center, thanks to the generosity of Mrs. Alger.

C-20 Rose Terrace.
Horace Trumbauer. 1934.
12 Lake Shore, Grosse Pointe Farms. (DN)

This Louis XV chateau, built for Mrs. Horace E. Dodge (1871-1970), is unquestionably Grosse Pointe's most regal residence.

C-21 Charles A. Dean House.
Hugh T. Keyes. 1924.
221 Lewiston, Grosse Pointe Farms. (MB)

Located on one of the few sloping sites in the area and surrounded by giant oak trees, this rambling Italian villa with its
red tile roof evokes memories of rural Tuscany.

C-22 Daniel W. Goodenough House.
Yamasaki & Girard. 1950.
234 Lothrop, Grosse Pointe Farms. (MB)

The T-shaped plan is on three levels. A small interior court
opens up the center of the house and the glass walls of the
living-dining area command a splendid view of towering pines.

C-23 Mrs. Henry Stephens House.
Charles A. Platt. 1913.
241 Lake Shore, Grosse Pointe Farms. (HHR)

The Flemish bonded brick of this French Baroque house are accented with stone trim and a graceful iron balcony on the central axis.

C-24 Gilbert B. Pingree House.
Raymond Carey. 1931.
270 Voltaire Pl., Grosse Pointe Farms. (MB)

Evoking souvenirs of the Old South, the Pingree house rises proudly between twin dependencies.

C-25 Sidney T. Miller Jr. House.
Robert O. Derrick. 1925.
248 Provencal, Grosse Pointe Farms. (HAL)

Partly painted brick and partly shingled, it recalls quaint old New England dwellings.

C-26 Country Club of Detroit.
Smith, Hinchman & Grylls. 1926.
220 Country Club Dr., Grosse Pointe Farms. (GPH)

The original *Kahn*-designed building was destroyed by fire in 1925, but *Smith, Hinchman & Grylls* resumed in very much the same "English Cottage" style. Notwithstanding its storybook romanticism, the design is tastefully executed. The rambling plan, large rooms, long connecting gallery, and broad window areas make a cheerful and pleasant gathering place for social activities.

C-27 Roy D. Chapin House.
John R. Pope. 1927.
457 Lake Shore, Grosse Pointe Farms. (DN)

A stately Georgian mansion with a comfortable as well as handsome interior.

C-28 Emory W. Clark House.
Hugh T. Keyes. 1934.
635 Lake Shore, Grosse Pointe Shores. (MB)

Set in beautifully landscaped grounds, the Clark house has the appearance of some venerable English country seat. The bow-fronted wings with delicate iron window guards give the house a late 18th century character foreshadowing the Regency style.

C-29 Joseph B. Schlotman House.
Albert H. Spahr. 1915.
501 Lake Shore, Grosse Pointe Shores. (MB)

C-30 Grosse Pointe Yacht Club.
Guy Lowell. 1927.
Lake Shore at Vernier, Grosse Pointe Shores. (JPM)

Here the romanticism of the 1920's came to a climax, rising out of the waters of Lake St. Clair like a vision of Venice, replete with campanile, Gothic window tracery, and arcaded loggia.

C-31 W. Hawkins Ferry House.
Meathe, Kessler & Assoc. 1964.
874 Lake Shore, Grosse Pointe Shores. (BK)

To take maximum advantage of a view on Lake St. Clair, a 2-story house was desirable. A modular system of precast concrete columns 15½ feet on center was used. All columns are exposed, exterior and interior, and concrete floors are supported on steel beams. On the east side, glass walls face a series of terraces descending to the lake. A 7-foot overhang shields the house from the sun. The living room and library, both 2 stories high, create an effect of spaciousness, and a balcony reached by a handsome spiral staircase adds to the number of vantage points from which dramatic views may be enjoyed. The house affords an ideal setting for the owner's collection of contemporary art.

C-32 Eastland Center.
Victor Gruen Assoc. 1957.
Eight Mile & Vernier Rds., Harper Woods. (JLH)

In many ways similar to Northland; however, the clients had learned much from their experience there, and consequently more emphasis was placed on sculpture, one court was enlarged for public gatherings, and a 6-story medical building was included in the project.

C-33 Alvan Macauley House.
Albert Kahn Assoc. 1929.
735 Lake Shore, Grosse Pointe Shores. (MB)

In a splendid setting of sweeping lawns, the massing and proportions of this Cotswolds inspired mansion give it the air of a great landed estate.

C-34 Edsel B. Ford House.
Albert Kahn Assoc. 1927.
1100 Lake Shore, Grosse Pointe Shores. (TE)

Having roamed the English Cotswolds with his father, Edsel Ford too fell under the spell of the local architecture. The same thoughtful skill and attention to details were employed by Jens Jensen in creating the landscaped setting as *Kahn* gave to the house itself.

D. North Side and Highland Park

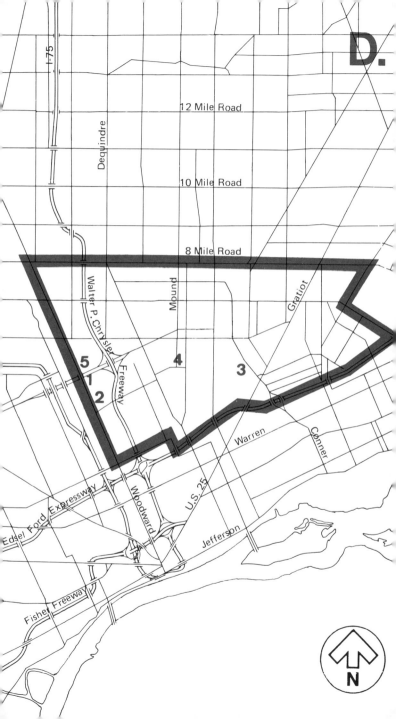

D-1 McGregor Public Library.
Tilton & Githens and *Burrowes & Eurich*. 1926.
12244 Woodward, Highland Park. (BHC)

One of the most attractive classical buildings in the Detroit area.
An unusual feature is the location of the book stacks in the basement, making the entire main floor available for public use.

D-2 Most Blessed Sacrament R. C. Cathedral.
Henry A. Walsh. 1915.
Woodward & Belmont. (MB)

An example of full-blown Norman Gothic, the twin towers dominate the vast cruciform structure. Stone groined vaults and tall clerestory windows filled with tracery create an imposing interior. The towers were completed by *Diehl & Diehl* (1951).

D-3 City Airport Terminal.
Albert Kahn Assoc. 1966.
11499 Conner. (L-A)

In this reinforced concrete structure the second floor metal and glass curtain wall provides a maximum view of the airport and is canted outward to minimize glare from the runways and paving, as well as to reduce exposure to direct sunlight.

D-4 Charles Terrace.
O'Dell, Hewlett & Luckenbach. 1940.
Mound & Sobieski. (FPH)

An early project to provide refuge in outlying areas for slum families, influenced by "International Style" massive European housing projects.

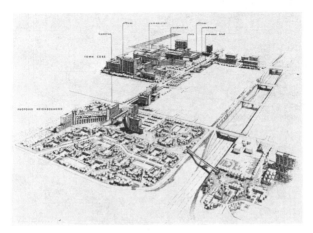

D-5 Highland Park Town Development.
Tarapata-MacMahon-Paulsen Assoc. 1968. (TMP)

A complex community of about 40,000 and, together with adjacent Hamtramck, entirely surrounded by Detroit, Highland Park has all the problems of a city of 400,000. (Now partially dismantled, in its day *Albert Kahn's* 1909-1914 Ford Highland Park Plant on Woodward Ave. turned out many of some 15 million Model T's; his 1910-1914 Dodge Bros. Corp. Plant in Hamtramck has been owned by Chrysler Corp. since 1928.)

The primary task of urban renewal — to improve the environment — could not be effected without altering local attitudes by breaking down traditional fears and hostility toward physical change. To achieve this the architects involved residents — in effect made them consultants — from the beginning of the planning process, and residential redevelopment had first priority.

Prefabricated temporary dwellings were planned for housing displaced families during the transitional period. A renovated and revitalized City Center is the focus of the total city plan. While this is not a completed environmental plan, or even one that will necessarily be realized, it is professional work at a very important scale.

E. Northwest Detroit

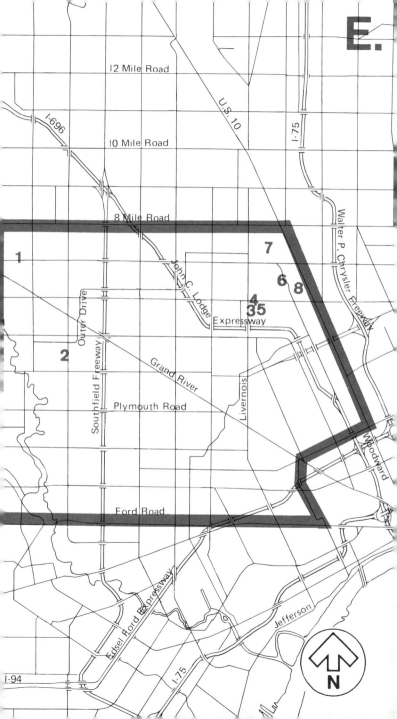

E.

E-1 American Concrete Institute.
Yamasaki, Leinweber & Assoc. 1958.
22400 W. Seven Mile Rd. (BK)

A small 1-story rectangular building with offices on either side of a central skylighted corridor. A precast concrete folded plate roof is cantilevered out from the corridor walls and extended over the windows of the exterior walls. End walls are screens made up of concrete pipe sections; spandrel panels and pierced grilles for the basement windows are precast concrete, and a low surrounding wall is of faceted concrete blocks.

E-2 John W. Smith Homes.
Lyndon & Smith. 1942.
Evergreen & Kendall. (MB)

A public housing project on the far northwest side suggesting the Bauhaus in the crisp mechanical precision of line. The architects experimented with plywood for exterior walls which, due to maintenance problems, were later covered with siding and asbestos shingles.

E-3 Fisher Administrative Center.
Gunnar Birkerts & Assoc. 1966.
University of Detroit Campus. (BK)

Divided into 3 elements: ground floor podium, 4 office floors,
and penthouse with executive offices and conference rooms.
Projecting columns in gray slate, blending with the dark tinted
glass of the window areas, support the floors. The roof is
suspended from the center core by concrete-encased cables.

E-4 University Center Annex.
Tarapata-MacMahon-Paulsen Assoc. 1970.
University of Detroit Campus. (BK)

Construction is reinforced concrete and exterior wall surfaces are lightly sandblasted; non-structural walls are of foot-square reddish brown brick. Continuous skylights introduce natural light along interior walls on the upper level. The north and west walls are glazed with solar bronze glass.

E-5 Ford Life Sciences Building.
Glen Paulsen & Assoc. 1967.
University of Detroit Campus. (HB)

A monumental effect is created with plain brick walls and projecting stair towers. Since interior classrooms are reached by peripheral corridors, minimal window area was required. This is the first of 6 laboratory buildings, adaptable to any science discipline. Others will be of varying height and connected by enclosed links. An adjoining low lecture hall classroom unit also serves as a university conference center.

E-6 Detroit Golf Club.
Albert Kahn Assoc. 1917.
17911 Hamilton. (MB)

Fine brickwork, banks of windows, and an interesting treatment of roof masses combine to make a pleasing and original "English Cottage" design.

E-7 S. Brooks Barron House.
Yamasaki, Leinweber & Assoc. 1955.
19631 Argyle Crescent. (H-B)

The charm of the house stems from the intimate relation between interior and outdoor areas—reflecting pool, Japanese rock garden, and sweeping lawn. A skylight brightens the center of the house.

E-8 Merrill Fountain.
Carrère & Hastings. 1901.
Palmer Park. (BHC)

Lizzie Merrill Palmer, wife of Senator Thomas W. Palmer, honored her father, lumberman Charles Merrill, with this fountain. Originally located in Campus Martius in front of the Detroit Opera House, *George D. Mason* (1898) (razed; see A-28) it was later moved to a more idyllic setting in Palmer Park.

In 1893 Senator and Mrs. Palmer gave Palmer Park to the city. It consisted of 130 acres carved from the 725-acre Palmer estate and was laid out in 1870 on a mildly undulating wooded tract. In 1895 the Palmers added to this gift a log cabin and the surrounding grounds, designed by Mrs. Palmer in 1882 as their summer residence. The city purchased an additional 147 acres in 1920 (see also B-42).

F. South Side and Dearborn

Ford Museum and Greenfield Village

Founded by Ford in 1929 as a museum of American history, the Henry Ford Museum and Greenfield Village contain one of the great collections of Americana and trace 3 centuries of American life in the development of its art and skills.

The museum building is 450 x 800 feet. Incorporated in the Georgian facade are full-scale reproductions of Independence Hall, Congress Hall, and Old City Hall in Philadelphia. Harvard handmade red brick, Cold Springs gray granite, a blue-gray Georgian marble, and soapstone were used to reproduce exactly the appearance of the originals.

Exhibits are arranged in the following general sections: American Decorative Arts, Street of Early American Shops, Mechanical Arts, and Henry Ford Personal History.

Greenfield Village, an adjunct to the Ford Museum, is a collection of some 100 buildings of historic interest moved from their original sites. Old-fashioned mills, stores, and dwellings, maintained as they were several generations ago, recapture the flavor of an earlier America. One of Ford's first, and appropriate, relocation and restoration was the white frame house in which he was born on 30 July 1863.

F-1 Henry Ford Museum.
Robert O. Derrick. 1929.
Village Rd. & Oakwood Blvd., Dearborn. (HFM)

F-2 Henry Ford Birthplace.
c. 1860.
Greenfield Village, Dearborn. (PH/HFM)

F-3 Ford Fairlane Towers.
Rossetti Assoc. 1972.
Gildow & Southfield, Dearborn. (RA)

The initial buildings of Ford Motor Co.'s 2,300-acre Fairlane development are these twin towers, 15-story commercial office buildings, thematic structures designed to set the basic aesthetics for an entire office park on a virtually virgin site. Each tower contains 260,000 square feet. They are linked by a first level plaza of about 30,000 square feet containing a bank, restaurants, and other service facilities.

The project was named for Henry Ford's Victorian style mansion, started by *Hermann von Holst*, a *Frank Lloyd Wright* associate, but completed by *William H. Van Tine* (1915). It overlooks River Rouge, not far away.

F-4 Ford Motor Co. Administrative Center.
Skidmore, Owings & Merrill. 1956.
American Rd. near Michigan, Dearborn. (FMC)

Consisting of an 11-story main building and the 6-story Lincoln Mercury Building, separated by the low slab of the parking garage, these towers loom above flat farmlands. Columns were placed outside the line of the curtain walls and inside the utility core to clear office spaces of obstructions. Since there was plenty of area, escalators were installed to relieve congestion in elevators. The building is a model of efficiency and striking evidence of the post-war trend toward decentralization.

F-5 Ford Division Building, Ford Motor Co.
Welton Becket & Assoc. and *Albert Kahn Assoc.* 1954.
17101 Rotunda Dr., Dearborn. (H-B)

F-6 River Rouge Plant, Ford Motor Co.
Albert Kahn Assoc. 1917-1938.
3001 Miller Rd., Dearborn. (FMC)

Begun in 1915 on a 2,000-acre farm near Detroit, the River
Rouge Plant developed unexpectedly when Ford was assigned
to manufacture Eagle Boats during World War I. He thought ship-
building would go faster inside than by the normal outdoor
construction technique and decided to use assembly line
methods developed at Highland Park. This called for unprece-
dented scale in construction. *Kahn* rose to the occasion with a
half-mile long structure. Wasting no time on architectural nice-
ties, he employed a steel frame with broad spans and walls
that were unbroken expanses of glass. Through later remodeling
and additions the River Rouge plant became the great autono-
mous industrial complex that has earned it the reputation of
being one of the marvels of 20th century America.

F-7 Marathon Oil Building.
Birkerts & Straub. 1962.
15911 Wyoming, Dearborn. (BK)

This office building is sheathed in matte-finish gray porcelain to minimize the effect of air pollution. Projections on the panels hold panes of dark gray glass, framed so that no bare metal is exposed to the corrosive atmosphere.

F-8 Fort Wayne Barracks.
Montgomery C. Meigs. 1848.
6053 W. Jefferson. (BHC)

A Georgian pile with Federal style overtones. The fort is now a military museum branch of the Detroit Historical Museum (in the Cultural Center on Woodward). No shot has ever been fired in anger from Fort Wayne.

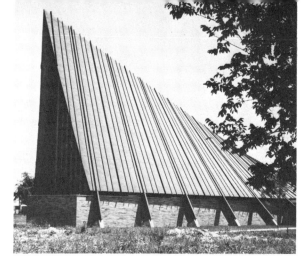

F-9 Christus Victor Lutheran Church.
Merritt, Cole & McCallum. 1964.
25535 Ford Rd., Dearborn Heights. (JPM)

Influenced by *Wright,* the architects placed a stained glass window behind the altar and covered the roof with copper.

F-10 Henry Ford Community College.
Eberle M. Smith Assoc. 1960.
5101 Evergreen, Dearborn. (L-A)

Operated by the Board of Education of Dearborn, and occupying a site given by the Ford Motor Co., the buildings have been grouped around a plaza. The largest one, containing classrooms and library, is constructed of concrete and faced with precast concrete panels.

Nearby are Dearborn Center of the University of Michigan, *Giffels & Rossetti* (1959), and Fair Lane, Henry Ford's home, *W. H. Van Tine* (1915).

F-11 Chrysler-De Soto Press Shop.
Albert Kahn Assoc. 1936.
McGraw & Wyoming. (H-B)

Widely acclaimed for the striking simplicity of its design, the press shop consists of a huge glass cage suspended from trusses.

G. Westland and Vicinity

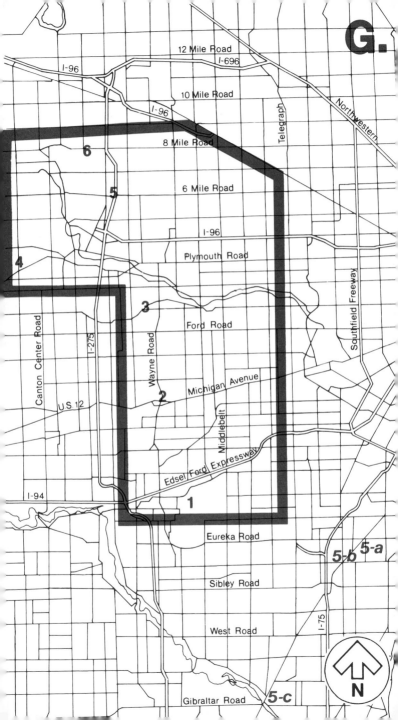

G.

12 Mile Road

I-96

I-696

10 Mile Road

I-96

Northwestern

8 Mile Road

6

6 Mile Road

5

Telegraph

I-96

Plymouth Road

4

Canton Center Road

I-275

Wayne Road

3

Ford Road

Southfield Freeway

U.S. 12

2

Michigan Avenue

Middlebelt

Edsel Ford Expressway

I-94

1

Eureka Road

5-a

5-b

Sibley Road

I-75

West Road

Gibraltar Road

5-c

N

G-1 Metropolitan Airport Terminal.
Smith, Hinchman & Grylls. 1966.
Near Romulus. (L-A)

According to the architects, this is the largest post-tensioned concrete structure in the world. Its bold functional forms capture some of the drama and excitement of the jet age. Horizontally curved beams on tapering cruciform columns support 5 huge concrete roof panels cantilevered out 35 feet over the access driveway.

G-2 Wayne Public Housing for the Elderly.
William Kessler & Assoc. 1969.
City of Wayne. (BK)

A deliberate attempt was made to orient 36 units inward to highly developed courtyards with an intimate atmosphere. Wood frame structures with cedar shingles were developed on 3 separate sites, and all units are identical 1-bedroom dwellings.

G-3 Westland Center.
Victor Gruen Assoc. and *Louis G. Redstone Assoc.* 1965.
35000 Warren, Westland. (BK)

Westland Center differs from *Gruen's* earlier shopping center projects by being contained under one roof, sheltered and air-conditioned. Fountains and sculpture add charm to large interior courts, and the controlled temperature encourages the growth of tropical vegetation.

G-4 Carl Wall House.
Frank Lloyd Wright. 1942.
12305 Beck, Plymouth. (WHF)

A glass-enclosed hexagonal living room with deep overhangs snuggles on top of a prow-like brick rampart overlooking a rolling countryside.

G-5 Schoolcraft College.

Eberle M. Smith Assoc. 1965.
19600 Haggerty, Livonia. (L-A)

Low brick buildings surround a quadrangle. Metal roofs with flaring eaves supported on laminated wood beams give character to the ensemble, and fieldstone retaining walls between grade levels add a rustic note.

G-6 Alan E. Schwartz House.

Birkerts & Straub. 1961.
40100 Eight Mile Rd., Northville. (BK)

Following the "much with little" philosophy of *Mies van der Rohe* is this square glass box. The surrounding raised deck is accessible through sliding glass doors from most rooms. Broad overhangs with deep fascias shade the interior and deck.

H. Southfield and Vicinity

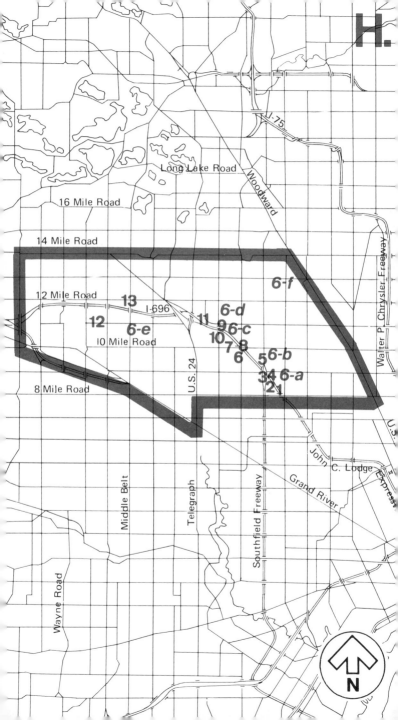

H.

Long Lake Road

Woodward

I-75

16 Mile Road

14 Mile Road

12 Mile Road

13

I-696

12

6-e

10 Mile Road

8 Mile Road

U.S. 24

11

6-d

9 6-c

10

7 8

6

5 6-b

3 4 6-a

2 1

6-f

Walter P. Chrysler Freeway

U.S.

John C. Lodge Expressway

Grand River

Southfield Freeway

Telegraph

Middle Belt

Wayne Road

N

H-1 Northland Center.

Victor Gruen Assoc. 1954.
Northwestern & Eight Mile Rd., Southfield. (JLH)

An inevitable result of the exodus to the suburbs of Detroit after World War II was the emergence of regional shopping centers. Their removal from arterial highways and their provision of adequate parking areas made these centers a distinct improvement over the earlier "strip" shopping areas. The largest and best planned centers in the metropolitan area are Northland, Eastland (C-32), and Westland (G-3), developed by the J. L. Hudson Co., the largest department store in Detroit.

Northland Center was *Gruen's* first regional shopping center and the first example in the country of "cluster" planning. Pedestrians are completely separated from automobiles. One-story stores, shops, markets, and restaurants are grouped around garden courts and pedestrian malls surrounding a 3-story Hudson store. This cluster of buildings is ringed by parking areas for 9,500 cars, and all trucking uses underground tunnels. One of the most popular features at Northland is the fanciful outdoor sculpture which, combined with music and flowers, gives the courts and malls the air of a foreign bazaar.

From the beginning, Northland Center was envisioned as the nucleus of a larger commercial area to be developed in a harmonious manner, and in recent years a hotel, a hospital, and office and apartment buildings have been constructed.

H-2 Reynolds Metals Building.
Minoru Yamasaki & Assoc. 1959.
16000 Northland Dr., Southfield. (BK)

A sales office for the Reynolds Aluminum Co., this building provided an opportunity to demonstrate the architectural possibilities of aluminum. The richness of its facade and roof line was a protest against the flatness and monotony of the curtain wall. With characteristic thought and care, *Yamasaki* created a building that is as fresh and original in its concept as it is in its details.

H-3 St. John Armenian Church.
Suren Pilafian. 1968.
22001 Northwestern, Southfield. (BC)

Built to commemorate the achievements and traditions of the flourishing period of church building in Armenia between the 4th and 14th centuries, the forms, materials, and design of this church recall the basic designs, ideas, elements, and philosophy of that millennium. These include the system of crossing semicircular arches to support a serrated conical gold-covered dome, blind arches, stone-framed doors and windows, ornamental stone carvings, and entrance portico with a belfry.

149

H-4 North Park Towers
Levine-Alpern & Assoc. and
Hirschfeld, Pawlan & Reinheimer. 1967.
16500 North Park Dr., Southfield. (B-K)

H-5 Congregation B'Nai David.
Sidney Eisenshtat & Assoc. 1966.
24350 Southfield Rd., Southfield. (JPM)

This square building, with 2 sweeping segmental arches springing from the corners on each side, encloses a cylindrical sanctuary, walled with a continuous stained glass window ranging in color from cool greens and blues to warm yellows and oranges.

H-6 Haley Funeral Home.
Birkerts & Straub. 1961.
24525 Northwestern, Southfield. (BK)

Steep hipped roofs are articulated to identify the locations of 3 major chapels, while the lobby, office, apartment, and service areas have low flat roofs to shade the walls. Projecting windows give the interiors a feeling of remoteness without complete isolation.

H-7 Lawrence Institute of Technology Project.
Earl W. Pellerin et al.
Northwestern & Ten Mile Rd., Southfield. (L-A)

Founded in 1932 by Russell Ellsworth and E. George Lawrence, on a site near the Ford Motor Co. Plant in Highland Park, as a non-profit institution, Lawrence Institute moved to its present 85-acre site in 1955. It offers 2- and 4-year courses in architecture, engineering, and industrial management, as well as arts and sciences. The campus buildings and master plan were designed (1970) under the direction of the chairman of the department of architecture.

H-8 American Office Park Development.
Rossen-Neumann Assoc. 1970.
Ten Mile Rd. & Northwestern, Southfield. (OCP)

A group of 3 rental office buildings arranged around a raised, tree-planted court. Building components are steel frame, exposed aggregate precast concrete, aluminum, and glass. Extremely large concrete panels allowed for rapid construction and a lively play of light and shadow.

H-9 **Allstate Building.**
Frederick Stickel Assoc. 1969.
Northwestern & Lahser, Southfield. (BK)

The quiet restraint of this finely detailed office building, planned around a large interior courtyard, offers a strong dependable corporate image. Dark aluminum and brick, mankato stone, and bronze glass define the exterior.

H-10 Federal-Mogul Corp. Staff Offices.
Giffels & Rossetti. 1966.
Northwestern & Lahser, Southfield. (L-A)

A 2-story steel and glass cage surrounded by a delicately tapered grid of precast prestressed concrete. The upper portion of the building hovers above an all-glass lobby and is supported by cast-in-place columns resting on a broad podium of textured concrete. Walls and columns in the lobby are faced with gray granite which contrasts pleasingly with red carpeting. The structure's lower level houses support facilities and is linked to the adjoining 2-story divisional office unit.

H-11 Congregation Shaarey Zedek.
Albert Kahn Assoc. and *Percival Goodman.* 1962.
27375 Adler Dr., Southfield. (BK)

With stained glass windows—symbolizing the burning bush—following the slope of the roof, the sanctuary juts out like a giant tent on a bluff overlooking Northwestern Highway.

H-12 Sisters of Mercy R. C. Novitiate Chapel.
Giffels & Rossetti. 1966.
28611 Eleven Mile Rd., near Quakertown. (JPM)

Dramatically commanding a bluff overlooking a lake, its narrow
stained glass windows behind the altar rise to the soaring peak
of the gable, bisecting a rugged fieldstone wall.

H-13 Arthur Beckwith House.
Meathe, Kessler & Assoc. 1960.
31765 Franklin Fairways, Farmington. (BK)

The saw-tooth roof pattern was derived from the practical
wooden A-frame truss construction, and the plan was based on
a series of 15-foot bays with exterior walls mainly of glass.

I. Birmingham and Vicinity

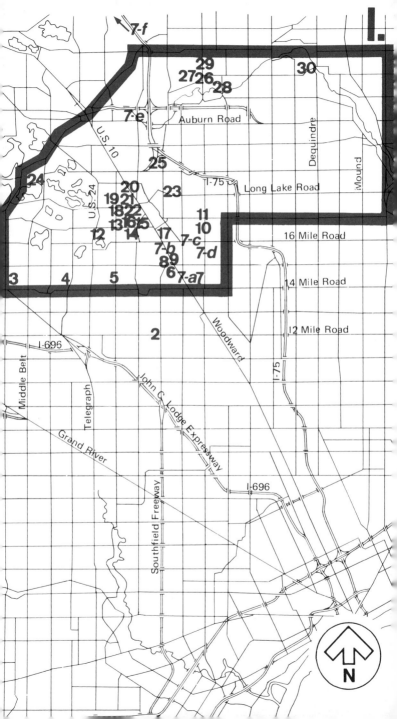

I-1 Orchard Ridge Campus, Oakland Community College.
Giffels & Rossetti and *Perkins & Will*. 1967.
27055 Orchard Lake Rd., Farmington. (GA)

A compactly grouped campus for 7,000 students. There are several large assembly rooms and an outdoor amphitheater seating about 1,000. The exterior treatment of exposed concrete, brick, and clay tile roofs offers positive articulation of various building forms.

I-2 St. Bede R. C. Church
Gunnar Birkerts & Assoc. 1969.
18300 W. Twelve Mile Rd., Southfield. (BK)

This addition to a school and church facility has a triangular plan to accommodate 1,500 and is based on the new liturgy concept. The fan-shaped roof extends toward the north light, focused onto the tabernacle placed in the main supporting column, where structural, visual, and philosophical concepts merge.

I-3 West Bloomfield Township Library.
Stickel, Jaroszewicz & Moody. 1963.
5030 Orchard Lake Rd., West Bloomfield. (L-A)

The library facility is a flat-roofed area with solid walls, while the room for civic and social gatherings is roofed with a triple barrel vault and faced with a glazed wall overlooking surrounding meadows. Wood beams and steel columns were left exposed.

I-4 Meadowlake Elementary School.
Linn Smith Assoc. 1963.
7100 Lindenmere Ct., Bloomfield. (L-A)

A continuous loop corridor circles a central block containing music rooms, library, kitchen, and multipurpose space; classrooms are placed outside the loop.

I-5 St. Regis R. C. Church.
Begrow & Brown. 1968.
3691 Lincoln Dr., Birmingham. (DB)

Part of a church-school complex. From a height of 48 feet the roof sweeps up to form a 100-foot tower designating the sanctuary, which a skylight at the tower's base floods with natural light.

I-6 101 Southfield Building.
O'Dell, Hewlett & Luckenbach. 1969.
Southfield & Maple, Birmingham. (BK)

A 3-story office building on a restricted site. The lower floor contains the main lobby and a covered parking area, the upper floors provide office space. The exterior of bronze-tinted glass and mahogany blends it into the residential community.

I-7 Our Shepherd Lutheran Church.
Glen Paulsen & Assoc. 1966.
2225 E. Fourteen Mile Rd., Birmingham. (BK)

Traditional in feeling without specifically resorting to traditional
forms, the unadorned interior wall surfaces and hidden light
sources epitomize spiritual values. The shed roof and the rugged
brick and wood textures create an atmosphere of austere
Nordic grandeur.

I-8 Willits West Town Houses.
O'Dell, Hewlett & Luckenbach. 1964.
Willits & Baldwin, Birmingham. (BK)

On a site of great natural beauty, these town houses satisfy the
needs of those no longer requiring large suburban homes but
for whom typical apartments offer too few amenities. Clusters of
6 single-family houses are compatible in scale, form, and
materials with neighboring homes.

161

I-9 Village Inn Motor Hotel.
O'Dell, Hewlett & Luckenbach. 1967.
300 N. Hunter Rd., Birmingham. (BK)

Acoustic privacy, of great concern to the builders of this luxury motor hotel on a busy highway, was provided by total concrete construction with brick veneer, forming an insulating cavity wall.

I-10 Somerset Fashion Mall.
Louis G. Redstone Assoc. 1969.
Big Beaver & Coolidge, Troy. (DB)

Some 30 high specialty shops are completely enclosed and air-conditioned.

I-11 First Citizens Bank of Troy.
Ziegelman & Ziegelman. 1970.
Big Beaver & Coolidge, Troy. (BK)

This newly organized bank opened 90 days after the architects were chosen. Six standard 12 x 37 foot modules were added to a central entrance and vault core.

I-12 Bloomfield Township Library.
Tarapata-MacMahon-Paulsen Assoc. 1969.
1090 Lone Pine Rd., Bloomfield. (BK)

To foster informality, warmth, and comfort, it is arranged in a village-like cluster of 4 steeply roofed pavilions. Laminated wood beams, placed diagonally over the reading areas, tend to reduce the visual scale of the rooms.

Cranbrook Institutions

In 1926 *Eliel Saarinen* was commissioned by newspaper publisher George G. Booth (A-26) to build an educational complex on his estate in Bloomfield Hills. The Cranbrook Foundation was organized the next year, and by 1943 the buildings were completed for its 4 institutions, now important factors in the cultural life of the area.

Booth was a pioneer in the development of suburban Bloomfield Hills and in 1918 built Cranbrook Meeting House to serve as a church and school. As the community grew, he foresaw the need for expanded educational and religious facilities. In view of his deep interest in art, it was natural for him to consider education in the arts essential.

At first Booth intended to convert his substantial farm buildings into a boys' school, but it soon became apparent that it would be easier to start from scratch. *Saarinen* then drew plans for a larger school, more or less following the lines of the original farm buildings. Opened in 1927, Cranbrook School consists of a number of brick buildings with steep red tile roofs, grouped around courts, and the general character of the work owes much to Scandinavian tradition. Wrought-iron work was done by Oscar Bach, sculptural ornamentation by Geza Maroti, a Hungarian *Saarinen* had known in Europe, and the quadrangle was enhanced with bronzes by Paul Manship and Carl Milles.

Immediately upon completion of the boys' school, plans for Cranbrook Academy of Art were developed with administrative offices, arts and crafts studios, and living quarters for faculty artists and students. In 1943 *Saarinen* completed the final building of the art academy, the art museum and library. Its severely plain walls and monumental portico serve as a background for fountains by Carl Milles.

Kingswood School for girls, completed in 1931, seems almost like a product of nature. The horizontal building masses conform to the sweep of the lake shore, while the copper roofs and pinkish-tan brick and stone blend in with the natural surroundings.

The year 1933 saw the completion of the Cranbrook Institute of Science. Its simple straightforward lines are reflected in a pool animated by playful Triton figures by Carl Milles.

I-13 Cranbrook House.
Albert Kahn Assoc. 1907.
500 Lone Pine Rd., Bloomfield Hills. (HC)

I-14 Christ P. E. Church Cranbrook.
Bertram G. Goodhue Assoc. 1928.
470 Church Rd., Bloomfield Hills. (CI/HC)

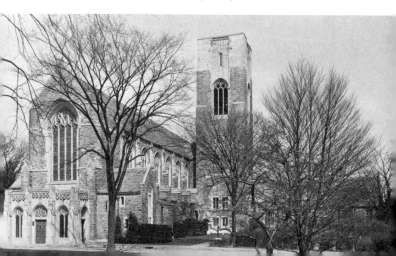

I-15 Cranbrook and Kingswood Schools.
Eliel Saarinen. 1927, 1931.
Bloomfield Hills. (HC)

I-16 Cranbrook Academy of Art.
Eliel Saarinen. 1943.
Bloomfield Hills. (CI)

I-17 Roeper City-Country School.
Tarapata-MacMahon-Paulsen Assoc. 1969.
2190 N. Woodward, Bloomfield Hills. (BK)

Constructed with a relatively new technique, called spiral generation, in which strips or planks of styrofoam, 4 or 6 inches thick, depending on dome size, are bent to conform to a circular foundation ring and fastened to it. Successive layers are built up and heat-welded to form a dome. Six 34-foot and two 37-foot domes house a unique educational program for 120 gifted pre-school children.

I-18 S. Gordon Saunders House.
Alden B. Dow Assoc. 1937.
1055 Orchard Ridge Rd., Bloomfield Hills. (ABD)

In the tradition of organic planning *Dow* inherited from *Frank Lloyd Wright,* plunging roofs and varying floor levels conform to the irregular topography and seem to express the prodigality of nature. A special feature is a pond at window-sill level which transmits its quivering reflections into the interior.

I-19 Bloomfield-Lahser Senior High School.
Tarapata-MacMahon-Paulsen Assoc. 1968.
3456 Lahser Rd., Bloomfield. (BK)

Construction is principally steel frame with exterior of face brick, tinted glass, and aluminum sash. The plan is organized into 3 academic houses clustered around a 21,000 square foot commons area containing a materials resource center.

I-20 Gregor Affleck House.
Frank Lloyd Wright. 1942.
1925 N. Woodward, Bloomfield Hills. (WHF)

Noting *Wright's* proclivity for building some of his most interesting houses on property nobody else wanted, Affleck chose a wooded lot traversed by a gully. The house juts out boldly from a hillside and seems to hover in the dense woodland.

I-21 Kirk-in-the-Hills.

Wirt Rowland and *George D. Mason & Co.* 1958.
1340 W. Long Lake Rd., Bloomfield. (BK)

The development of Gothic church architecture in the Detroit area came to a brilliant culmination with the completion of the Kirk-in-the-Hills, fulfilling Col. George's desire for a beautiful church that would serve the Bloomfield Hills community. Cedarholm is incorporated as a church house in the south facade.

I-22 Cedarholm.

George D. Mason & Co. 1923.
1340 W. Long Lake, Bloomfield. (GDM)

The rough slate roof with sagging ridge, clustered gables, and flowing roof lines gave the Edwin S. George House the pastoral character of an English countryside. The restraint and skill with which diverse elements were combined made it an outstanding example of the "Cottage Style."

I-23 **William B. Bachman House.**
Tarapata-MacMahon Assoc. 1963.
201 Lakewood Dr., Bloomfield Hills. (BK)

A large luxurious residence for an executive, designed for frequently entertaining large groups with formality and elegance.

I-24 **Our Lady of Orchard Lake R. C. Chapel.**
Walter J. Rozycki. 1963.
Commerce & Orchard Lake Rds., Orchard Lake. (JPM)

Following a *Victor Lundy* prototype, the roof arches of laminated wood are designed as quadrant segments of a circle, placed back-to-back to create pleasing upward curved lines. The projection of the copper roof serves as both entrance porch and canopy for an enormous statue of Our Lady of Orchard Lake by Clarence Van Duzer. The walls are of fieldstone.

I-25 Fox Hills Elementary School.
Begrow & Brown. 1969.
1661 Hunters Ridge Dr., Bloomfield. (DB)

One of the first schools with a completely open academic area, it has a peninsular walkway, extending from the main entrance to separate bus and auto traffic for greater safety.

Oakland University

In 1957 the late Mr. and Mrs. Alfred G. Wilson gave to the Board of Trustees of Michigan State University their Meadowbrook Farms estate and $2 million to assist in the foundation of a new university. The 16-acre estate included Meadowbrook Hall (I-28) and subsidiary buildings, and wooded and rolling land. Oakland University, as the new university is called, opened in September 1959 with 570 students; in 1971 the enrollment was almost 7,000. From the original 3 buildings, the campus has grown to 21.

I-26 Baldwin Pavilion.
O'Dell, Hewlett & Luckenbach. 1964.
Oakland University. (L-A)

Said to have the best acoustics for outdoor concerts in North America. It was designed as simply as possible to emphasize the natural setting, and can accommodate a maximum audience of 6,500.

I-27 Kresge Library.
Swanson Assoc. 1963.
Oakland University. (L-A)

Flexibly planned for an undefined library program, its only fixed element is a central service core.

I-28 Meadowbrook Hall.
Smith, Hinchman & Grylls. 1929.
480 S. Adams Rd., near Rochester. (L-A)

The main inspiration for Alfred G. and Matilda Wilson's sprawling baronial mansion was Compton Wynyates, a great 16th century Tudor manor house in Warwickshire. This is particularly evident in the entrance bay, with battlements and arch surmounted by a 3-light mullioned window, in the lofty twisted chimney-stacks, and in the charming exterior mingling of stone, brick, and half-timber work. The focal point of the vast interior is a spectacular 2-story ballroom. The staircase leading from the hall is a masterpiece of carving and design. Heraldic stained glass windows, an ornately carved pipe organ, and hand-rubbed paneling were removed from the same architects' 1920 Grosse Pointe Farms mansion of the late John F. Dodge, Mrs. Wilson's first husband.

I-29 St. John Fisher R. C. Chapel.
Swanson Assoc. 1966.
3665 Walton Blvd., near Rochester. (L-A)

Built to serve Oakland University, the form and plan were determined by a fan-shaped seating arrangement to bring the congregation close to the altar. This is one of the earliest churches designed to meet the requirements of the new liturgy. It is faced with hard-burned "clinker" brick; the roof rises from 24 feet at the baptistry to 40 feet over the sanctuary.

I-30 Beach House.
Wakely-Kushner Assoc. 1965.
Stony Creek Metropolitan Park. (BK)

The basic concept consists of 56 concrete "trees" with the building, comprised of precast aggregate panels, constructed underneath. In season it serves as many as 5,000 people a day.

J. Warren and Mount Clemens

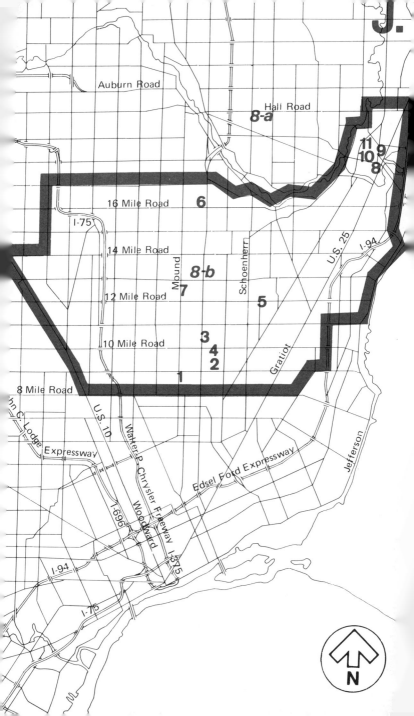

J-1 Chrysler-Dodge Half-Ton Truck Plant.
Albert Kahn Assoc. 1937.
21500 Mound Rd., Warren. (H-B)

The roof design was unique for its time. To provide better natural illumination, monitors hang down below the roof level instead of projecting above it.

J-2 Bundy Tubing Office Building.
William Kessler & Assoc. 1970.
12345 Nine Mile Rd., Warren. (BK)

To impart its industrial character to the building, limited corrosion steel tubes were used for both mechanical distribution lines and as forms for the reinforced concrete columns. Brown and bronze glass spandrel panels were used between tubes.

J-3 St. Clement R. C. Church.
Diehl & Diehl. 1961.
25320 Van Dyke Rd., Center Line. (BK)

It is perhaps no accident that one of the more technically advanced churches in the Detroit area is near the General Motors Technical Center (J-7). The structure consists of two thin intersecting parabolic shells of concrete rising directly from the ground. What makes St. Clement's unique is the method of construction; the concrete was pumped in place with a hose onto a form made of wood ribs covered with acoustical cement and wood fiber decking. When the concrete dried the form was left in place, and green sheet-aluminum roofing was applied on the exterior. The ends of the shells were then filled in with precast concrete window panels glazed with stained glass.

J-4 Kramer Homes School.
Saarinen, Swanson & Saarinen. 1942.
8830 Ten Mile Rd., Center Line. (WHF)

Built to accommodate defense workers who flocked to Detroit during World War II, 2-story row houses and 1-story semi-detached houses surround a central playground. The houses are of wood construction sheathed with redwood stained different colors. The well-designed school and community house are at the end of the playground.

J-5 Macomb County Community College.
Harley, Ellington, Cowin & Stirton. 1965.
14500 Twelve Mile Rd., Warren. (C-C)

Rows of similar buildings are joined by an arcade of shallow precast concrete arches around a quadrangle. The walls of the buildings themselves are composed of similar but taller arches, each filled with textured cinder-block panels surrounded by narrow window areas.

J-6 Chrysler Corp. Jet Engine Plant Test Cells.
Albert Kahn Assoc. 1951.
Sixteen Mile & Van Dyke Rds., Sterling Heights. (H-B)

General Motors Technical Center

It was Alfred P. Sloan Jr., president of the company, who launched the idea of combining in one place all the facilities for the General Motors technical staffs, then scattered all over the Detroit area. A site was acquired north of Detroit at Mound and Twelve Mile Rds. in Warren, and *Saarinen, Saarinen & Assoc.* were chosen as architects.

From the beginning *Eero Saarinen* was determined the architecture of the center should be expressed in the technical terms of the product to which it was dedicated. Like the automobile, the 25 buildings of the complex were composed mainly of steel, aluminum, and glass.

The construction of the center was begun in 1949. There are clusters of buildings for each of the 5 staff organizations: research, process development, engineering, styling, and service. The buildings are grouped in a landscaped setting around an artificial lake. Parking lots are hidden by shrubbery, and the entire complex is enclosed in a greenbelt of trees.

In this campus-like environment, so conducive to study and experimentation, *Saarinen* created a monument to the automotive age. He carried forward the tradition of industrial architecture established by *Albert Kahn* and gave it a new warmth and elegance. Here are the familiar long, low buildings with their interminable facades of glass, but to these were added end walls of vividly colored glazed bricks. In contrast to these rectilinear forms, the oval mass of a stainless steel water tower hovers above a lake and complements the gleaming dome of the Styling Auditorium at the opposite end of the lake.

Saarinen lavished the same care and attention upon the interiors of the buildings as he did upon the exteriors. In each of the principal lobbies there is a spectacular staircase, each distinctive in design, that provides a visual climax.

Like his father, the younger *Saarinen* also believed in enriching architecture with sculpture. "A sculptor," he said, "brings to a building his special sensitivity." In the central restaurant is a magnificent gilded screen by Harry Bertoia, and in front of the Styling Administration Building stands the monumental Bird in Flight by Antoine Pevsner. As a finishing touch, Alexander Calder created a water ballet with playing jets at the end of the lake. Small wonder the center has been called the "Versailles of Industry."

J-7 Styling Buildings.
Eero Saarinen & Assoc. and *Smith, Hinchman & Grylls*. 1956.
General Motors Technical Center, Warren. (GMC)

J-8 Mount Clemens Federal Savings Building.
Meathe, Kessler & Assoc. 1961.
77 S. Gratiot Ave., Mount Clemens. (BK)

One of the most glamorous of the innumerable branch banks resulting from the prosperity that followed World War II. The main structure is a thin-shell concrete roof supported on columns at the 4 corners. The space between the columns is filled with glass curtain walls, and the roof is pierced by a cluster of plastic skylights. Undulations in the roof give the building added strength, at the same time creating a dramatic effect.

J-9 Macomb County Building.
Ellis-Naeyaert Assoc. 1970.
40 N. Gratiot Ave., Mount Clemens. (GK)

A 6-story structure clad in precast concrete combined with bronze solar windows. Courtrooms are circular arenas where judges, litigants, attorneys, clerks, and juries interact.

J-10 Mount Clemens Public Housing I
Meathe, Kessler & Assoc. 1959. (BK)

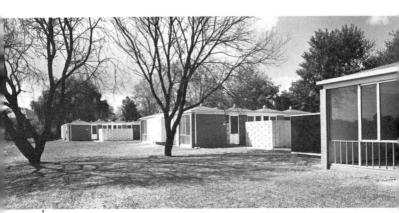

J-11 Mount Clemens Public Housing II
Meathe, Kessler & Assoc. 1969. (BK)

Two projects designed for the Housing Commission of Mount
Clemens. Housing I: 100 2-story units limited to not more than
4 in one building—all arranged to create pleasant tree-shaded
areas away from streets for child play and community activities.
Housing II: all 1-story units built on 60 scattered sites on typical
residential lots to provide a stimulus for upgrading adjacent
marginal dwellings as well as to eliminate specific identifica-
tion with a project development.

K. Ann Arbor and Vicinity

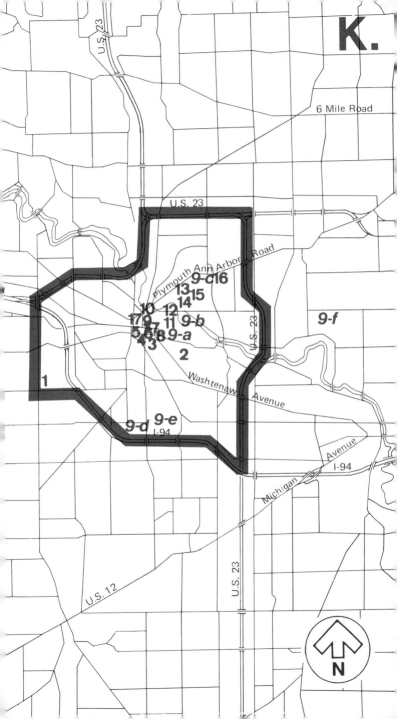

K.

6 Mile Road

U.S. 23

Plymouth Ann Arbor Road

9-c 16

13
14 15

10 12
17 9 9-b
8 7 11
5 6 8 9-a
4 3
2

9-f

U.S. 23

1

Washtenaw Avenue

9-d 9-e
I-94

Michigan Avenue I-94

U.S. 23

U.S. 12

N

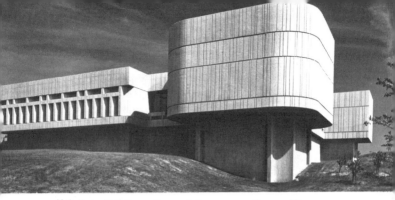

K-1 Detroit Edison Co. and Consumers Power Co.
Michigan Electric Pool Control Center.
Smith, Hinchman & Grylls. 1969.
Wagner & Scio Church Rds. (SHG)

This facility of approximately 17,000 square feet centralizes the generation and transmission of more than 10 million kilowatts of electrical power and will permit substantial energy exchange with utilities in Ohio and Indiana. The all-concrete building has its own fallout shelter and a generating station to provide non-interruptive service for computer and TV monitoring equipment. The first facility of its type, it is completely separated from other facilities of the participating utility companies.

K-2 Towsley House.
Alden B. Dow Assoc. 1932.
1000 Berkshire. (ABD)

Said to be the first residence designed with attached garage facing the street.

University of Michigan

In 1817 Judge Augustus B. Woodward drew up an educational plan which was adopted as law by the governors of Michigan Territory. Woodward named it the Catholepistemiad or University of Michigania. John Monteith, a Presbyterian minister, was appointed president, and Father Gabriel Richard, a Roman Catholic priest, vice president. The scheme was too elaborate and advanced for the Detroit of its day, so the legislative council abolished the Catholepistemiad and established the University of Michigan in 1821, but there was no real university until Michigan became a state in 1837. At that time the question of where to locate the university was solved when the growing community of Ann Arbor offered a 40-acre tract.

The Board of Regents erected a college building and 4 professors' houses, one of which, several times enlarged and remodeled, survives as the President's House. The buildings were completed in 1841, and the first class—7 students—was admitted by a faculty of 3. Though enrollment slowly increased during the first decade, the university remained merely a small country college with a curriculum based on the classics and mathematics, and after 1850, medicine.

In 1850 Michigan adopted a new constitution which provided for direct election by the people of the regents of the university and gave them entire control of its affairs. The state constitution also provided that the regents elect a president and Henry Philip Tappan was inaugurated in 1852. Under his leadership a scientific course and civil engineering were introduced, elective courses were permitted, advanced study was encouraged, and outstanding men were called to the faculty. An observatory and a chemical laboratory were erected, and the Law School was instituted. In 1870 Michigan became the first large university to admit women and the first to admit freshmen on their high school diplomas.

By 1871 when James Burrill Angell became president, Michigan was the largest university in the United States. A diplomat as well as a scholar, Angell's impact on the university was possibly the greatest of any single individual; 50 buildings were constructed during his 38-year tenure.

Between 1909 and 1920, under Harry Burns Hutchens' presidency, 114 parcels of land were added to the campus by gift, purchase or condemnation, but the university remained intolerably overcrowded, and the first major expansion did not come until 1950 when Harlan H. Hatcher was president. The regents purchased land north of the Huron River for a North Campus, which is now 887 acres. The next decade saw the greatest building pace ever experienced. A branch of the university was opened in Flint in 1956, another in Dearborn in 1959. With enrollment exceeding 38,000 in 17 schools and colleges, the campus covers 1,216 acres in the city, plus 1,107 acres in the area.

K-3 William L. Clements Library.
Albert Kahn Assoc. 1923.
University of Michigan. (H-B)

This jewel-like building was given to the university by Clements to house his distinguished collection of rare Americana. It is said *Kahn* stated he desired most of all to be known as the architect of this building.

K-4 Regents Plaza.
Johnson, Johnson & Roy. 1968.
University of Michigan. (M)

The Michigan Union, left, *Pond & Pond;* Administration Building, right, *Alden B. Dow Assoc.* (1968). Sculpture in the center is by Bernard Rosenthal.

K-5 General Library.
Albert Kahn Assoc. 1919.
University of Michigan. (HAL)

Colored terracotta spandrel medallions and frieze provide accents against fine brickwork.

K-6 Institute for Social Research.
Alden B. Dow Assoc. 1966.
University of Michigan. (H-B)

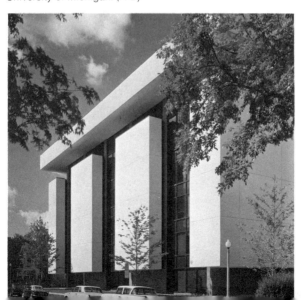

191

K-7 Angell Hall.
Albert Kahn Assoc. 1922.
University of Michigan. (FS)

Kahn's admiration for his friend *Henry Bacon's* Lincoln Memorial in Washington more than likely inspired the imposing portico with its 8 massive Doric columns.

K-8 Physics and Astronomy Building.
Albert Kahn Assoc. 1963.
University of Michigan. (BK)

K-9 Hill Auditorium.
Albert Kahn Assoc. 1913.
University of Michigan. (H-B)

A rich veneer of brick and tile provides a contrasting frame for a monumental stone entrance colonnade.

K-10 C. S. Mott Children's Hospital.
Albert Kahn Assoc. 1969.
University of Michigan. (FS)

K-11 University Reformed Church.
Birkerts & Straub. 1961.
100 E. Huron, Ann Arbor. (BK)

A feature is the natural light admitted through deep, rectangular cells of uniform size and detail at each setback, and through skylights at the edge of the roof. The concrete exterior is painted a warm gray; the interior is white. The only other architectural material in the nave is wood. Red brick is introduced in the narthex for transition to future wings and courtyards.

K-12 Towsley Center for Continuing Medical Education.
Alden B. Dow Assoc. 1969.
University of Michigan. (BK)

K-13 Vera Baits Student Housing.
Swanson Assoc. 1965.
North Campus, U.M. (L-A)

Intimate and selective rooms for upper class and graduate students.

K-14 School of Music Building.
Eero Saarinen & Assoc. 1964.
North Campus, U.M. (UM)

The planes and units of the building exemplify *Saarinen's* insistence that a structure harmonize with its surroundings, without seeming to grow from them. Situated beside a small lake in wooded hills, this is the only building on the campus designed by *Eero*, although his firm was retained as consultants for overall planning of the North Campus.

K-15 North Commons.
Swanson Assoc. 1965.
North Campus, U.M. (L-A)

K-16 Climax Molybdenum Co. of Michigan.
Smith, Hinchman & Grylls. 1965.
1600 Huron Pkwy. (BK)

The initial buildings in this complex are grouped around 3 sides of a landscaped court, to be closed in the next phase. The steel framing is filled with precast concrete panels, and wall panels are either solid or glazed, as interior use dictates. A deep cornice/fascia houses mechanical and electrical distribution systems.

K-17 Main Street Promenade.
Johnson, Johnson & Roy. 1967.
Main St., Ann Arbor. (JJR)

This pedestrian mall provides for traffic and on-street parking while introducing trees, paving, and street furniture to create a unified streetscape in an area of widely differing building facades.

Detroit
Architecture
1971–1980

(Note: Date cited after architect's name indicates year of project's completion or anticipated completion.)

1. Downtown Detroit

Please refer to map on p. 21.

1-a Renaissance Center.
John Portman & Assoc. 1977.
Jefferson between Randolph & Beaubien. (BK)

Renaissance Center was initiated by Henry Ford II, who formed the Renaissance Center Partnership of 51 corporations to revive the failing downtown in 1971. The $350 million first phase is possibly the world's largest privately financed real estate development.

The Center's height is 741 feet above Jefferson Avenue. The 1,400 room Detroit Plaza Hotel is 73 stories high, topped by the world's largest revolving restaurant. Its 8-story atrium lobby includes a ½-acre reflecting pool and is laced by 5 levels of aerial walkways. Four 39-story office towers will be joined by two 21-story towers in 1981. One hundred shops comprise the retail area in the 4-level podium for the towers.

The skylights in the complex cover 2 acres. The building's surface contains another 46 acres of glass. The project generated more than $1 billion in economic growth for downtown Detroit in its first year of operation.

1-b Detroit/Windsor Tunnel Plaza.
Ellis/Naeyaert/Genheimer Assoc., Inc. 1979.
Jefferson & Randolph. (ENG)

The Detroit/Windsor Tunnel was built in 1930. The recent renovation of the tunnel plaza complex includes new toll and immigration facilities, a tunnel bus station, a duty-free store, plus an office building to house customs, immigration, and tunnel company operations.

**1-c Horace E. Dodge & Son Memorial Fountain.
Philip A. Hart Plaza.**
Isamu Noguchi. 1979.
Smith, Hinchman & Grylls, Consultants.
Jefferson & Woodward. (BK)

This center for Detroit's successful ethnic festival series and an
array of special events was launched by the bequest of Mrs.
Dodge for the obelisk at the edge of the site. The fountain, which
is programmed for changing water and light configurations,
marks the peak of *Noguchi's* (a native of Arizona) international
reputation.

1-d Detroit Federal Savings and Loan Association Headquarters.
T. Rogvoy Assoc. 1971.
511 Woodward. (TR)

Constructed on a site "left over" from an earlier widening of Woodward, the building extends to the property limits in all direction, giving it a depth of only 30 feet. The reflective glass exterior makes this building a recognizable element despite the overwhelming size and individuality of the neighboring buildings.

1-e Beaubien House (Michigan Society of Architects).
Unknown Architect, ca. 1851. Restoration, 1981.
553 E. Jefferson. (BK)

One of Detroit's oldest remaining houses is now headquarters for the Michigan Society of Architects. At one time, some 15 similar Italianate townhouses were located in the area until epidemic "parking lot-itis" struck in the 1950's. The sturdy wood structure of the modest 7-room house has made it an ideal candidate for restoration as one of the last examples of period residential architecture in the core city.

1-f University of Detroit Law School Library.
Smith, Hinchman & Grylls. 1977.
651 E. Jefferson. (DB)

The expansion and renovation of Dowling Hall (A-36) represents the commitment of the Law School to its downtown location, near city, county, and federal courts. The brick and stone facade of the library blends with the existing building. Its major features are a landscaped entrance, courtyard, and a 3-story, skylit student lounge.

1-g Frank Murphy Hall of Justice.
Eberle M. Smith Assoc. 1968.
Gratiot & Walter P. Chrysler Freeway. (BK)

The 12-story quarters for Detroit's Recorder's Court contains 22 court suites and office and detention facilities. The landscaping of the plaza adjacent to the building is an especially fine example of Detroit's renewed awareness of the importance of the pedestrian's environment.

1-h Michigan Bell Telephone Main Office Building

Smith, Hinchman & Grylls. 1974.
Michigan Ave. & Cass. (BK)

The 17-story building's stepped-back configuration is derived from the pie shape of the site of MBT's original headquarters. The granite and glass structure is designed to accept a 9-story future addition to its height. The massive sculpture "Jeune Fille et Sa Suite," located on the southeast corner of the site, was executed by Alexander Calder.

1-i Patrick V. McNamara Federal Building.
Smith, Hinchman & Grylls. 1976.
Michigan Ave. & Cass. (BK)

The 1.2 million square foot building is the largest single-tenant office building in Detroit, consolidating some 5,000 federal employees previously dispersed throughout the downtown area. The 27-story reinforced concrete building has corners which have been recessed for better distribution of structural loads. Parking for 250 cars is provided in a 5-level garage beneath the outer edge of the site.

1-j Washington Boulevard Plaza.
Rossetti Assoc. 1979.
Washington Blvd. between Grand Circus Park & Michigan Ave. (BK)

The 5 block long series of plazas, pools, fountains, and plantings is designed for relaxation, entertainment, and dining. One of the Motor City's most grand avenues is now given over to exclusively pedestrian use, with the exception of a vintage trolley.

1-k Smith, Hinchman & Grylls Building.
Smith, Hinchman & Grylls. 1910/1972.
455 Fort St. (BK)

Among the first of a wave of wholesale renovations of older buildings in Detroit during the seventies. The structure was stripped to its reinforced concrete frame and rebuilt to modern standards. The exterior wall system on the north and west elevations is of bronze-tinted glass in a specially designed aluminum framing system.

1-l Joe Louis Sports Arena.
Smith, Hinchman & Grylls. 1980.
651 E. Jefferson. (SHG)

The Joe Louis Sports Arena adds a striking new element to Detroit's skyline. West of the Cobo Hall Convention Center, the arena is linked to adjacent parking and surrounding facilities by elevated and grade level walkways. The arena seats 21,000 patrons; a private club and 61 suites are located on a separate loge level. An interior corridor circles the arena, giving access to all seating areas.

A unique structural design, the arena roof is supported by 2 trusses, 58 feet apart. Each is 40 feet deep and spans 441 feet. A floor between the trusses contains a second private club/restaurant.

2. Inner City

Please refer to map on p. 57.

2-a Calvary Baptist Church.
Gunnar Birkerts & Assoc. 1977.
Lafayette & McDougall. (GB)

The building is in a park-like setting which extends from the neighboring Elmwood Cemetery. The building's yellow-orange ribbed metal manifests the happy and hopeful attitude of this congregation. The strong, simple form is superscale sculpture. Inside, an immense, faceted mirrored wall allows the congregation to observe the service and the choir (placed in a recess in the wall) from every point in the seating area.

2-b Fort Street Instructional Center, Wayne County Community College.
Sims, Varner & Assoc.; Giffels Assoc. 1979.
Fort St. & John C. Lodge Expressway. (GCM)

A new 3-story classroom and laboratory center with child-care and parking facilities is connected to a former railroad freight house that has been stripped to its structural frame and converted to a learning resource center. The old and new buildings are bridged by an enclosed commons that negotiates a 14-foot drop in the site's elevation.

2-c State of Michigan Plaza Building.
Jickling, Lyman & Powell. 1972-1975.
Howard & Brooklyn. (JK)

This building was originally conceived as the Detroit Trade Center by a consortium of private developers. Designed to be a tenant-occupied office building, the center later was expanded and subsequently occupied by the State to consolidate its operations in the Detroit area.

2-d Southwest Detroit Hospital.
Eberle M. Smith Assoc. 1975.
Michigan Ave. & 20th St. (BK)

This hospital was created by the merger of 4 existing small hospitals in southwest Detroit. The multi-story nursing tower is planned to nearly double in size. The building's materials were selected for lightness due to low bearing capacity of the soil and to resist industrial fumes generated nearby.

**2-e General Lectures Building,
Manoogian Hall,
Wayne State University.**
Jickling, Lyman & Powell. 1971.
Beckett, Jackson & Raeder, Landscape Architects.
Warren & Third. (RCP)

The plaza developed between these two academic halls belies
the 20-foot diameter city sewer that bisects the site and determined the placement of the buildings.

2-f Walter P. Reuther Library of Labor and Urban Affairs, Wayne State University.
O'Dell, Hewlett & Luckenbach. 1975.
Cass & Kirby. (BK)

This 4-story archives gathers reading, research, and office facilities around a skylighted atrium which provides public display space on the ground floor. Behind the atrium are stacks for books and documents, kept under controlled temperature and humidity conditions. The building is placed at a major pedestrian entrance to the campus as a memorial to Mr. Reuther.

217

2-g Second Avenue Mini Parks.
Johnson, Johnson & Roy. 1979.
Second & Grand Blvd. (JJR)

In the first phase of General Motor's revitalization of the New Center area, landscape improvements on Grand Boulevard and 2 urban parks were completed. In the second phase, 6 blocks of a residential area will be renovated to include a new office, retail and high-rise housing area.

2-h Detroit Science Center.
William Kessler & Assoc. 1979.
John R & Warren. (BK)

This building is the first phase of what may ultimately become one of the largest, most comprehensive science centers in the United States. A stainless steel box for exhibition space is supported above an underground space theater. The space theater and its escalator tubes are sheathed in bright red glazed tile to provide them with a special identity. Inside the escalator tubes, pulsating neon lights of bright colors promote excitement for the visitor proceeding to and from the space theater.

2-i Center for Creative Studies.
William Kessler & Assoc. 1975.
Robert M. Darvas & Assoc., Structural Engineers.
Kirby between John R & Brush. (BK)

This acclaimed design is based on a structural system that houses the building's mechanical linkages and can be rearranged and expanded to meet future requirements. The arrangement of the modules into the building's final form was the last step in the design process.

2-j Detroit General Hospital.
Wayne State University Health Care Institute.
William Kessler & Assoc.; Ziedler Partnerships; Giffels Assoc.
1979.
Medical Center. (BK)

The 5-story hospital and 9-story health care institute connect at
their 3 lower levels to share many facilities. Circulation patterns,
materials, and the use of color and light are keys to the architectural interest.

3. East Side and Grosse Pointe

Please refer to map on p. 91.

3-a Bon Secours Hospital.
Rossetti Assoc. 1976.
Cadieux & Jefferson. (BK)

The hospital is located in one of Grosse Pointe's finest residential areas. Consequently, the height, form, and material of its expansion and renovation were handled with restraint and sensitivity to reflect the neighborhood setting.

**3-b Ambulatory and Critical Care Building,
Clinical Office Building.
Saint John Hospital.**
Smith, Hinchman & Grylls. 1979.
Moross & Chandler Park Dr.

The dominant center for advanced medical care in its area,
these facilities are the first phase of a large expansion program.
The original main building has already been expanded and renovated under earlier programs. The challenge in the new construction has been to soften the impact of the massive scale on
the adjacent residential neighborhoods.

4. South Side and Dearborn

Please refer to map on p. 131.

4-a Detroit Automobile Inter-Insurance Exchange Headquarters.
Giffels Assoc. 1974.
Ford Rd. near Southfield Freeway. (GA)

The gridded appearance of the AAA building is created by energy-saving sunscreens. The 5 stair towers connect the 3 floors on the exterior so that the interior is uninterrupted in its 600-foot length. Within this space, office furnishings are arranged with screens, plants, and graphics in place of walls.

4-b Fairlane Town Center.
The Taubman Co., Developer. 1976.
Southfield Freeway & Michigan Ave. (DB)

Five of six planned major stores and approximately 218 shops
occupy Fairlane's 1.5 million square feet of leaseable space. The
center is the commercial core of the Ford Motor Land Development Corporation's 3½ square mile planned development. An
elevated people-mover system connects the mall to the Hyatt
Regency Hotel.

4-c Hyatt Regency Dearborn.
Charles Luckman & Assoc. 1976.
Southfield Freeway & Michigan Ave. (HRD)

The Hyatt Regency program of dramatic interior forms and spaces is maintained in this 12-story, 800-room hotel, which was expanded in 1979 to provide increased guest accommodations and amenities. The automatically controlled transportation (people-mover system) connects the hotel to Fairlane Town Center.

4-d J. Walter Thompson Building.
Alden B. Dow Assoc. 1975.
Southfield Freeway near Ford Rd.

Earth berms screen parking and reduce the mass of this office
building. The advertising agency's offices and studios open to a
3-story atrium lobby used for special events and exhibits.

5. Southwestern Suburbs

Please refer to map on p. 141.

5-a Security Bank & Trust Co. Headquarters.
Eberle M. Smith Assoc. 1972.
Trenton Rd. & Fort St., Southgate. (BK)

This 14-story office building for bank operations and lease space locates elevators, stairs, and services on the end towers so that interior spaces are free for general offices.

5-b Wayne County Mental Retardation Center.
Eberle M. Smith Assoc. 1975.
Pennsylvania Rd., east of Allen Rd., Southgate. (L-A)

Designed as a grouping of residential scale buildings to create a neighborhood setting, the center is home, school, and a treatment facility for 150 residents.

5-c Flat Rock Municipal Building.
O'Dell, Hewlett & Luckenbach. 1975.
Evergreen Rd. & Gibraltar Rd., Flat Rock. (OHL)

This municipal center accommodates city offices, police and fire station, city jail, and council chamber within a single 3-story building. Connecting the various parts of the building is a 2-story gallery with a curved ceiling that reflects the roof profile. The owner wished the building to reestablish civic awareness in a community that had been swallowed in suburban sprawl. The building's industrial style expresses the community's dependence upon nearby industrial development.

6. Southfield and Vicinity

Please refer to map on p. 147.

6-a Southfield Campus,
Oakland Community College.
Straub, VanDine, Dziurman. 1980.
Rutland Dr. near Nine Mile Rd., Southfield. (DB)

One of the first examples of underground architecture in the area, this complex responds to natural elements to provide a campus feeling in an urban setting. It complements the surrounding community of high-rises by preserving as much natural outdoor space as possible.

6-b IBM Office Building.
Gunnar Birkerts & Assoc. 1979.
Nine Mile Rd. & Southfield Freeway, Southfield. (BK)

Energy conservation, the principal ideal behind the design of this building, is symbolized by the changing exterior wall color. A bright, natural aluminum on the south and west reflects heat from the sun where it is the most powerful. The darker gray color on the north and east similarly absorbs heat. Specially designed windows are shielded for most of the work day, brightening the interior with reflected rather than direct sunlight.

6-d Bendix World Headquarters.
Rossetti Assoc. 1978.
Civic Center Dr. near I-696, Southfield. (BK)

The original headquarters and a recent expansion are complementary in their scale, use of materials, and detailing. Open office spaces and a dramatic atrium have been enhanced by Louise Nevelson's sculpture "Trilogy."

239

6-c Prudential Town Center.
Neuhaus & Taylor. 1976-1979.
I-696 near Civic Center Dr., Southfield. (G-P)

The first phase of this $250 million development was the 32-story
golden-glassed tower recognizable by its exposed X-bracing.
The low-rise retail building, parking structure, and plant-filled
theme building were followed by the second phase's 20-story
tower with rounded ends.

6-e American Center Tower.

Smith, Hinchman & Grylls. 1976.
Franklin Rd. near Eleven Mile Rd., Southfield. (BK)

Twenty-six stories of offices rise from the 3-story service, commercial, and parking base. The glass tower is double-glazed to conserve energy while retaining the spectacular view over the countryside in this growing suburban area. Although it is the headquarters for American Motors, a substantial number of the office floors are leased to other tenants.

6-f William Beaumont Hospital.
Smith, Hinchman & Grylls. 1976 (Addition).
Thirteen Mile Rd. near Woodward, Royal Oak. (BK)

This hospital has established an extraordinary reputation for advanced medical care. The 9-story addition raises its capacity to 910 beds and increases diagnostic and treatment services. The architectural detailing of the addition is unusually successful in relating to the original structure, so that the entire complex gives the appearance of having been constructed at the same time.

7. Birmingham, Troy and Vicinity

Please refer to map on p. 157.

7-a 555 South Woodward.
O'Dell, Hewlett & Luckenbach. 1975.
Woodward & Hunter Blvd., Birmingham. (BK)

The 16-story apartment tower of this multiple-use complex
heralds the southerly approach to central Birmingham. The tower
(containing 99 apartments) and a 3-level office block to the north
rise above a 3-story parking platform and 2 levels of retail shops.
The shops open onto a sheltered promenade and a pair of sunk-
en plazas facing Woodward Avenue.

7-b Great American Building.
Rossetti Assoc. 1976.
Woodward & Oakland, Birmingham. (DB)

The 4-story office/commercial building features a 4-level interior lightwell. The sawtooth north facade accommodates the curving border road for maximum use of the irregular site.

7-c Troy Place Office Center.
Rossen/Neumann Assoc. 1974-1979.
Big Beaver & Coolidge, Troy. (BK)

The 5 buildings in this largest office complex in Troy vary in height from 1 to 7 stories. The buildings feature large expanses of energy-efficient bronze reflective glass and brick entries. It was constructed in 5 phases from 1974 to 1979 and houses a Detroit Edison district office, the Sperry Univac Building, and headquarters for Ex-Cell-O, the Budd Company, Borg-Warner, and First Citizens Bank.

7-d Top of Troy.
Rossetti Assoc. 1976.
Big Beaver & I-75, Troy. (BK)

A 25-story triangular office tower and 2 retail levels are placed to create a landscaped plaza. The tower's facade changes in relation to its solar orientation.

7-e Pontiac Silverdome.
O'Dell, Hewlett & Luckenbach. 1975-1976.
Opdyke Rd. & M-59, Pontiac. (BK, exterior; L-A, interior)

The largest air-supported roof structure in the world covers the 80,600-seat Pontiac Silverdome, designed primarily for Detroit Lions football games. The whole roof assembly of Teflon-coated fiberglass on a network of steel cables weighs less than 1 pound per square foot, and is held aloft by inside air pressure of about 4 pounds per square foot above atmospheric pressure. Between the upper and lower seating levels is a "Club" level with about 100 private boxes. From all levels spectators can exit directly outside onto ramps on earth berms beside the building.

247

7-f Pine Knob Music Theater.
Rossen/Neumann Assoc. 1972.
Sashebaw Rd., Independence Township. (BK)

Designed both for musical presentations and Broadway plays, the theater seats 5,360 under the 60,000 square foot roof, with lawn seating for an additional 5,000. The trusses, the longest items ever shipped anywhere in Michigan, are 140 feet long with 50-foot cantilevers. A carnival quality is achieved by super graphics in orange and red throughout.

8. Macomb County Suburbs

Please refer to map on p. 177.

8-a Lakeside.
The Taubman Co., Developer. 1976.
M-59 & Schoenherr, Sterling Heights. (DB)

Approximately 187 shops and 5 major stores occupy the mall's 1½ million square feet. The interior contains a grand court, performing arts area, year-round ice arena, and a 4-screen movie theater. Residual commercial and residential development includes 2 man-made lakes and a wooded island park.

8-b Macomb County Satellite Services Building.
Thomas Strat & Assoc. 1977.
Van Dyke near Thirteen Mile Rd., Warren. (DB)

The glass wall of the triangular building is the solar collector for
one of the state's largest active solar heating and cooling systems. Computer analysis was used in developing the design of
the building as well as its energy system.

9. Ann Arbor and Vicinity

Please refer to map on p. 187.

9-a Federal Building.
TMP Assoc. 1977.
Liberty & Fifth, Ann Arbor. (H-B)

The 4-story, general office building steps back at every level to present a low profile suited to the pedestrian traffic between downtown and the University of Michigan campus. A system of skylights draws natural light into the building without creating large solar heat gains.

9-b Law School Library Addition, University of Michigan.
Gunnar Birkerts & Assoc. 1981.
Monroe & Tappan, Ann Arbor. (GB)

The Law School at the University of Michigan is a self-contained unit with its own dormitories, dining hall, library, and social areas, built in the 1920's in a pseudo-Gothic style. The underground addition preserves the integrity of the original complex. The plan wraps the existing library structure and connects into the existing library. A deep trough opens the underground to the outside and reflects light into the interior of the new space. The top of the structure is earth-covered with lawn and low plantings.

9-c Bentley Historical Library. 1973.
Gerald R. Ford Presidential Library. 1980.
Jickling, Lyman & Powell.
North Campus, University of Michigan. (BK)

The manuscript library includes many special features necessary to the unique requirements for the processing, preserving, and displaying of rare and important documents. The 1977 donation of papers by former President Ford justified the design of a separate building connected to the original library.

9-d Briarwood.
The Taubman Co., Developer. 1973.
S. State St. & Eisenhower Blvd., Ann Arbor. (DB)

The first of the Taubman Company's 4 regional retail developments in southeastern Michigan contains nearly a million square feet of leasable space. The 128 shops and 4 major stores are complemented by amenities that include a performing arts area, a 4-screen movie theater, and a community room.

255

9-e Wolverine Tower.
Rossetti Assoc. 1974.
State Rd. & I-96, Ann Arbor. (DB)

The scale and warm colors of the glass, steel, and masonry 10-story office makes it a focal point of a rapidly growing commercial area on Ann Arbor's outskirts.

9-f Washtenaw Community College.

TMP Assoc. 1976.
4800 E. Huron River Dr., Ann Arbor. (BK)

Located on 235 rolling, wooded acres, the campus links academic buildings by enclosed galleries, bridges, and passages which form an internal street. To date, the Learning Resource Center, Exact Sciences Building, and Technical and Industrial Building have been completed. All buildings are planned on a 5-foot grid to accommodate integrated systems for ceilings, lighting, air handling, and partitions.

Index of Illustrations

(Names of architects and architectural firms are in italics. Designations beginning with a letter indicate projects begun or completed through 1971; those beginning with a number indicate projects begun or completed after 1971.)

259